FEARON'S

Biology

SECOND EDITION

FEARON'S
Biology
SECOND EDITION

Lucy Jane Bledsoe

Globe Fearon Educational Publisher
Paramus, New Jersey

Paramount Publishing

Pacemaker Curriculum Advisor: Stephen C. Larsen
Stephen C. Larsen holds a B.S. and an M.S. in Speech Pathology from the University of Nebraska at Omaha, and an Ed.D. in Learning Disabilities from the University of Kansas. In the course of his career, Dr. Larsen has worked in the Teacher Corps on a Nebraska Indian Reservation, as a Fulbright senior lecturer in Portugal and Spain, and as a speech pathologist in the public schools. A full professor at the University of Texas at Austin, he has nearly twenty years' experience as a teacher trainer on the university level. He is the author of sixty journal articles, three textbooks, and six widely used standardized tests, including the Test of Written Learning (TOWL) and the Test of Adolescent Language (TOAL).

Subject Area Consultant: Jack Coakley
Jack Coakley holds a B.S. in Bacteriology and Immunology from the University of California, Berkeley. He is currently teaching science at El Cerrito High School, El Cerrito, California.

Editor: Stephen Feinstein
Contributing Editors: Sharon Wheeler, Steven Kloepfer
Production Editor: Teresa Holden
Cover Design: Mark Ong, Side by Side Studios
Text Design: Dianne Platner
Illustrations: Duane Bibby

About the Cover Photograph: *Art Wolfe, All Stock.* Penguins are one of the hardier lifeforms on our planet, able to withstand extremely cold temperatures and harsh living conditions. They are also one of the few birds that cannot fly, having lost that ability in the evolutionary process. To find out more about penguins and other ware-blooded vertebrates, see Chapter 14.

Other photos: Harold Wes Pratt/Biological Photo Service 2, 52; Paul W. Johnson/Biological Photo Service 26, 74; Photo Researchers, Inc. 38, 182; The BETTMANN NEWSPHOTOS 62; Biological Photo Service 92; Frank Siteman/Jeroboam, Inc. 112, 254; AP/Wide World Photos, 121, 273; Jane Scherr/Jeroboam, Inc. 124; Vince Compagnone/Claremont Courier/Jeroboam, Inc. 136; Kent Reno/Jeroboam, Inc. 150; Suzanne Arms/Jeroboam, Inc. 164; Walter Down/Photo Researchers, Inc. 194; George Whiteley/Photo Researchers, Inc. 208; Rose Skytta/Jeroboam, Inc. 218; David Parker/Photo Researchers, Inc. 230; UPI/BETTMANN NEWSPHOTOS 242; Emilio Mercado/Jeroboam, Inc. 264; John K. Nakata/Terraphotographics/Biological Photo Service 274; T.W. Ransom/Biological Photo Service 288; Ken Gaghan/Jeroboam, Inc. 304.

Other photos courtesy of: Foster Farms/Hill & Knowlton, Inc. 14; Woodbridge Metcalf/Save-The-Redwoods League 102.

ISBN 0–8224–6890–5

Printed in the United States of America

3. 10 9 8 7 6 5 4 3 2
Cover Printer/NEBC
DO

Contents

A Note to the Student

In another fifty years, will people get jobs working on asteroids? Why aren't there any dinosaurs alive today? Is a virus a living thing, like a germ, or a nonliving thing, like a chemical? Is the Earth getting so warm that the polar ice caps might melt? How would that affect people's lives?

Biology is the science of life. By studying living things—and how they relate to one another—biologists try to answer questions like these. Advances in life science can lead to better lives for all people on Earth. Knowledge of biology can help us fight off diseases. It can show us how to clean up our air and water. It can help athletes become stronger and faster. And it can protect plants and animals from extinction.

Knowing something about biology is in your own interest. As you read this, rain forests are being cut down in South America. Somewhere oil is being spilled into the ocean. These things may be happening thousands of miles away. But they affect you and every other creature on Earth who needs to breathe air and drink water. As we enter the twenty-first century, some important choices will have to be made. What do we have to do to protect our environment? Only people who understand the basic concepts of biology will be able to make wise decisions.

Further study of biology can prepare you for an interesting career. Perhaps you would like to work in a hospital, a zoo, or a research laboratory. Perhaps you are interested in farming or fishing or teaching. These are just a few of the job opportunities in this field of science.

Look for the notes in the margins of the pages. These friendly notes are there to make you stop and think. Sometimes they comment on the material you are learning. Sometimes they give examples. Sometimes they remind you of something you already know.

You will also find several study aids in the book. At the beginning of every chapter, you'll find **Learning Objectives**. Take a moment to study these goals. They will help you focus on the important points covered in the chapter. **Words to Know** will give you a look at some science vocabulary you'll find in your reading. And at the end of each chapter, a **summary** will give you a quick review of what you've just learned.

We hope you enjoy reading about life science. Everyone who put this book together worked hard to make it interesting as well as useful. The rest is up to you. We wish you well in your studies. Our success is in your accomplishment.

Science Comes to Life

Chapter 1

The Science of Living Things

When the oceans first formed, there was no life on Earth. For millions of years, the sea covered most of the Earth's surface. Then, something amazing happened: the first specks of life appeared in the oceans.

Chapter Learning Objectives

- Explain the difference between a theory and a fact.
- Name the five steps in the scientific method.
- Name the five fields of biology.
- Name two jobs you could have by studying biology.

Words to Know

biology   the study of living things

botany   the study of plants

characteristics   the qualities of a living thing that make it unique

control   a known quantity by which to measure the subject of an experiment

ecology   the study of how all living things relate to one another and their world

environment   everything in the immediate world around you

experiment   a test to get information

fact   an idea that has been proven by experiments

genetics   the study of how the characteristics of a living thing are passed along to its offspring

microbiology   the study of living things too small to be seen with the naked eye

offspring   the young of a living thing

theory   an idea that has not been proven with experiments

universe   everything that exists, including the Earth, sun, planets, stars, and outer space

zoology   the study of animals

Billions of years ago, a great cloud of gas and dust formed in the **universe.** This cloud became denser and denser. Then, about 4-1/2 billion years ago, the dense cloud became a planet. Today we call that planet Earth.

Over millions of years, mountains thrust up and oceans washed over the land. Glaciers moved down from the mountains and then back up again. Great storms tore across the Earth.

Millions of years passed. Then, slowly, tiny green specks appeared in the oceans. These green specks were the first life on Earth.

Life Science Is the Study of Living Things

The stars, mountains, drops of water, and the human brain are all subjects of science. Science is the study of the whole universe. In this book you will study only one field of science. You will study living things: from the first green specks to your own brain. The study of living things is called *life science* or **biology**.

The first living things probably appeared in the oceans. These living things were nothing more than tiny green specks. They did not think. They did not do much of anything but live and grow.

Over time, these green specks changed. Some changed into fish. Others changed into plants. Some of the fish crawled out of the oceans. There they changed into land animals. Each of these changes took many, many years. People were among the last new life forms to appear on Earth.

In this chapter you will learn about the five fields of biology. You will learn how biologists go about their work. You will also read about some jobs in biology.

These first specks of life were very simple and very small. You couldn't see them with the naked eye.

The study of living things is called life science or biology. The study of non-living things is called physical science.

The Beginning of Life Science

No one knows who the first biologist was. But one thing is sure: biology, like all science, began with questions.

Imagine this . . .

You are a member of an early tribe of humans. You wander around hunting for animals. You eat the meat. You use the skins for clothing. You gather fruits and plants for food, too.

You know that animals are alive like you. After all, they walk, sleep, and eat. You may even know that plants are alive. You see that they grow and make seeds.

One day, a storm sweeps in. Great winds rush through your camp. Bolts of lightning strike trees and start fires.

You wonder if the wind is some kind of living creature, too. It moves like a herd of wild animals. And it roars like a fierce animal.

In some ways, the fire also acts like a living thing. After all, it grows, it eats trees, and after a while, it dies. Is the fire alive? You're not sure.

The early people on Earth probably asked these questions. Of course, they did not know that these were scientific questions.

But all science starts with questions. "Is it alive?" is the first question of biology.

As you read this book, be sure to ask questions about anything you don't understand.

Experimenting to Find Answers

An **experiment** is a test to get information. People have always experimented. Those early humans may have tried to touch fire. They were looking for information. No doubt they discovered that fire is hot.

This experiment probably helped them figure out that they could use fire to cook food. They could also use it to warm their camps.

Today, all scientists use experiments to test their ideas. When experiments prove an idea to be true, the idea is known as a **fact**.

Some ideas are based on a lot of good information. But they have not been proven with experiments. These ideas are called **theories**.

Some ideas in science must remain theories forever. For example, there are theories about how the universe began. But there are no experiments that can ever prove these theories. It would be necessary to make another universe!

People in Biology: Kent Cullers

Kent Cullers has been blind since birth. He has never seen the moon or a star. Yet the idea that there might be life somewhere out there in space has always fired his imagination. Cullers works with other scientists who are using radio waves to search for intelligent life in the universe. He has designed a computer program that can interpret radio signals coming from outer space.

Cullers believes if intelligent beings in space are sending out signals, there would be a pattern to the radio waves. The computer can tell the difference between a noisy hiss and a real message. Someday Cullers' computer program may detect signals from another planet.

Biology Practice

Write answers to these questions on a separate sheet of paper.

1. What is biology?
2. Which of the following are studied by life scientists?

   a. rocks   d. lightning

   b. snakes   e. spiders

   c. trees   f. snow
3. Why do scientists need to do experiments?

The Scientific Method

Scientists today follow a special set of steps in their thinking. These steps are called the *scientific method*. This way of thinking is at the center of all modern science.

Here are the five main steps in the scientific method:

1. Ask a question.
2. Gather information.
3. Suggest a good answer to the question.
4. Test your answer with experiments.
5. Draw conclusions.

Suppose you wish to buy a new car. You want to make sure it is better than your old car. Use the scientific method to help you make a good choice.

1. **Ask a question**. Which car should I buy?

2. **Gather information**. You might begin by talking to some friends about their cars. What do they like? What do they dislike? You might ask specific questions, such as how fast do the

Gathering information is also called doing research. *Scientists do research to prepare their experiments.*

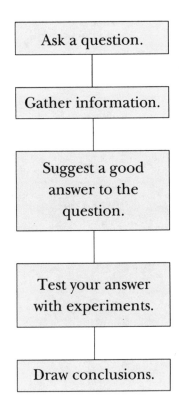

Ask a question.

Gather information.

Suggest a good answer to the question.

Test your answer with experiments.

Draw conclusions.

Flow chart of scientific method

An experiment proves the theory only if you get the same result each time you do it.

cars go? What kind of gas mileage do they get? How often do the cars need tune-ups or repairs? Do they give a comfortable ride?

Next, you might go to a car dealer, or a mechanic, and ask about the new cars. You could read articles in automobile or consumer magazines. And you could look at all the advertisements.

Let's say they all tell you that the new foreign import, the Vroom, is the best. Then you ask your automobile association. It says the same thing. The Vroom is the car to get.

3. **Suggest a good answer to the question**. It certainly appears the Vroom is the car you want.

You could stop right here. After all, everyone says the Vroom is the best. They all say it is better than your car. Several magazine articles have supported their opinion. But a car is a very important purchase. You want to be sure. You need to find out for yourself. So you proceed to step four in the scientific method.

4. **Test your answer with experiments**. You go to the foreign car dealership and ask to test drive a Vroom. You take it out for a test drive. You compare it to your car. You compare its handling. You check its gas mileage against your car's gas mileage. You test both cars in the city and on the freeway. In this experiment, your old car is the **control**. A control is something you already know everything about.

It is a known quantity by which to measure the subject of your experiment. In this case, you are measuring the qualities of the Vroom against the qualities of your old car. You compare them in any way that will give a meaningful result. A meaningful result is one that will prove or disprove what you have learned of the Vroom. You might take notes to suggest further experiments.

5. **Drawing conclusions**. Now is the time to draw conclusions. If you took notes, you will want to study them. Is the Vroom the best car for you on the market?

If this were a real scientific study, you would want to write up a report. That way other scientists could benefit from your work. In the case of the Vroom, you might want to tell your friends about your experiments. After all, they all want to have the best car, too.

Different Fields of Biology

"Life" is a huge topic. Most biologists choose one area in which to specialize. Five important areas of biology are botany, zoology, genetics, microbiology, and ecology.

Botany is the study of plants. **Zoology** is the study of animals. **Genetics** is the study of how life's **characteristics** are passed along to **offspring**. Much of this work is done in science laboratories, better known as "labs." Often these labs are in universities. Sometimes they are in private companies. **Microbiology** is the study of living things too small to be seen with the naked eye. "Micro" means small.

You will be studying a lot more about each of these fields of biology. For now, just try to understand the main ideas.

Microbiologists use microscopes to study tiny living things. This work is also done in labs most of the time. **Ecology** is the study of how all living things interact with one another and with the non-living world.

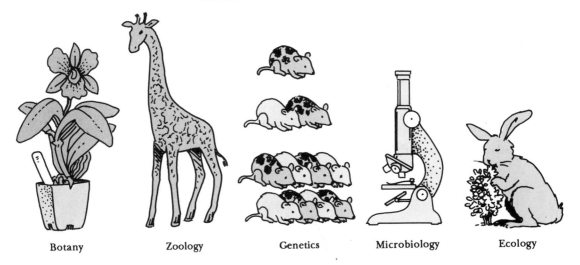

Botany   Zoology   Genetics   Microbiology   Ecology

The branches of biology

Jobs in Life Science

Biologists work in all kinds of places. Some work on ships. These biologists might study fish and plants in the sea. Some work in zoos. There are jobs studying and caring for animals in the zoo. Some biologists work as veterinarians or veterinary assistants.

Farmers must know a great deal about growing plants. They often employ botanists to help them grow better crops. Large nurseries hire botanists to improve their plants. Botanists work for city, state, and national parks. They study the plants and trees that grow there. They help to keep the plants healthy.

Many cities and states hire ecologists to make sure the **environment** stays in balance. Ecologists check on the work of industries. They make sure these industries are not breaking laws protecting the environment.

There are also many biology jobs in the field of health care. All doctors and nurses must know a great deal about biology. The people who work in laboratories in hospitals also must know biology.

Appendix A at the back of this book lists many of the jobs in life science. Appendix B lists some of the places that hire biologists.

Chapter Review

Chapter Summary

- The study of living things is called biology.

- All science starts with questions. Answers to these questions are tested with experiments.

- Some biological ideas have not yet or cannot be proven by experiment. These ideas are called theories.

- Scientists today use the scientific method to study problems. There are five steps to the scientific method:

  1. Ask a question.

  2. Gather information.

  3. Suggest a good answer to the question.

  4. Test your answer with experiments.

  5. Draw conclusions.

- Botany is the study of plants.

- Zoology is the study of animals.

- Genetics is the study of how the characteristics of living things are passed along to offspring.

- Microbiology is the study of living things too small to be seen by the naked eye.

- There are many, many jobs in life science. People with training in biology can work on boats, in parks, on farms, in hospitals, for industry, government, and businesses.

Chapter Quiz

Write the answers to the following questions on a separate sheet of paper.

1. Where did the first living things probably appear?
2. Why might people living many years ago have thought fire was alive?
3. What must happen for a theory to become a fact?
4. What are the five steps in the scientific method?
5. Suppose you wanted to gather information about different kinds of potatoes. List two places you could go to find this kind of information.
6. Why do scientists write up reports explaining their conclusions from experiments?
7. The study of blackberry bushes is in which of the five fields of biology?
8. The study of the eating habits of dogs is in which field of biology?
9. What does a botanist study?
10. Name three jobs in life science.

Jobs in Life Science

Look at the list of careers in biology in Appendix A at the back of the book. Choose a job that interests you. On a separate sheet of paper, write two things about the job you would like.

Mad Scientist Challenge: Experimenting

Imagine you are living on Earth thousands of years ago. You begin experimenting with a sharp rock. What kinds of things might you discover? What uses do you think you can make of the rock? Write your answer on a separate sheet of paper.

Chapter 2

Being Alive

You are surrounded by living things. But how do you know they are alive? It's not always easy to tell. What do living things do that non-living things cannot do?

Chapter Learning Objectives

- Define and explain what an organism is.
- Name the six important characteristics of life.
- Describe what happens to the bodies of organisms after they die.

Words to Know

cell the tiny basic units of which all living things are made

decay to break down into smaller pieces

energy the ability to do work

microscope a device for viewing objects that are too small to be seen with the naked eye

microscopic something too small to be seen with the naked eye

nutrients the substances in foods that organisms need for energy

organism any living thing

recycle to use again

reproduction the way organisms make more of their own kind

respond to act according to conditions in the environment

wastes the leftover matter a cell or body does not need after it uses food for energy

Think of all the ways you are different from a rock. A rock cannot run across a field. It cannot eat a sandwich. It cannot talk. It does not grow. You could probably think of a hundred other differences between you and a rock. The biggest difference between you and a rock is that you are *alive*.

In Chapter 1, you read that the first question in biology is: "Is it alive?" In this chapter you will learn what it means to be alive.

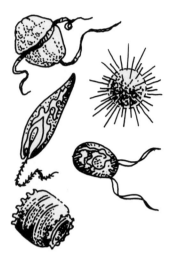

Single-cell organisms

Living Things Are Called Organisms

Anything that is alive is called an **organism**. Bushes, turtles, rats, grasses, fish, and trees are all organisms. You are an organism.

The biggest organism on Earth is the blue whale. This animal is so big that its heart is the size of a small car. Its tongue alone weighs about three tons—as much as a truck.

Most of the organisms on Earth cannot be seen with the naked eye. Billions and billions of tiny creatures live in the sea, on land, even on your body. These tiny organisms are **microscopic**. That means they are so small you must use a **microscope** to see them.

It may seem as if the blue whale and a microscopic organism have nothing in common. But they are both alive. That means they have six very important things in common.

All organisms 1) can move on their own; 2) reproduce; 3) use energy; 4) grow; 5) respond to their environment; 6) are made of cells. The rest of this chapter will explain these six characteristics.

Movement

You can kick a rock across a street. But a rock cannot roll across a street on its own. Only living things can move on their own. If a thing cannot move on its own, it is not alive.

Animals move for reasons. They move to find food. They move to get out of strong sunlight. They move to find mates. They move to get away from danger. Or they move for fun, as people do when they dance. Animals fly, swim, walk, run, and crawl.

Plants also move on their own. They move a lot more slowly than animals, however. Think of a flower. In the morning, when the sun comes out, that flower will open up. When the sky grows dark again, the flower closes up.

Plants move toward sunlight. If you have any house plants, take a good look at them. Chances are, the leaves have turned toward the window. The house plant itself even leans toward the window.

Why do you think plants move toward sunlight? You will learn all about this in Unit 3.

Reproduction

All organisms give birth to offspring. Offspring are new organisms that come from grown ones. Babies are human offspring. Puppies are the offspring of dogs. Seedlings are the offspring of plants.

Organisms make more of their own kind by a process called **reproduction**. All living things reproduce. Some simple kinds of organisms reproduce by splitting in two. In more complex organisms, two members of the same species are needed for reproduction. Usually one of these organisms is a female and one is a male.

On the Cutting Edge

The common cold, AIDS, and many other diseases are caused by a tiny thing called a *virus*. Scientists do not agree about what a virus is. Some say it is a living organism. Others say that a virus is a non-living thing.

Why all the confusion? Because sometimes viruses act like living things. Other times they do not. For example, viruses cannot reproduce on their own. But they like to invade organisms. Once inside an organism, a virus reproduces much like a living thing.

Many biologists are working to understand viruses better. Perhaps in your lifetime, they will find a way to control viruses.

Using Energy

You may feel completely at rest when you are sitting in front of the TV. In fact, parts of you are hard at **work**. Your brain is busy taking information from the TV. Your heart is pumping blood through your body. Your lungs are taking in oxygen and letting out other gases. You are using up **energy** even as you sit still.

That is why you must eat. Food gives you energy to do work. The more work you do, the more food you need.

Even when you are asleep, you are using energy. Your lungs still breathe, and your heart continues to pump blood.

All living things use energy. That means they all need food. Some animals hunt other animals for food. Some animals eat plants. Still other animals eat both plants and animals.

Plants also do work and use energy. You cannot see plants working unless you use a special camera. But their roots are busy taking up water and nutrients from the soil. The leaves of plants are soaking up sunlight. And special chemicals in the leaves are turning sunlight into food.

Organisms do not use all the food they take in for energy. They must process the food for the **nutrients**. Nutrients are the parts of the food that give them energy. But there are always parts of the food that organisms cannot process for energy. These are called **wastes**. Plants and animals alike must dispose of these wastes.

Biology Practice

Make two lists on a separate sheet of paper. At the top of the first list, write "Using Energy." Then list at least five ways you have used energy today. Circle the two things that you think used the most energy.

At the top of the other list, write "Getting Energy." Write at least five things you have eaten to get energy today. Circle the two foods that you think gave you the most energy.

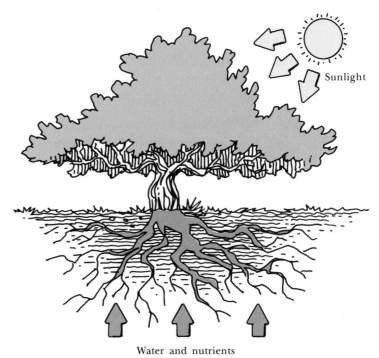

Sunlight

Water and nutrients

Plants need sunlight, water, and nutrients from the soil in order to grow.

Growth

All living things grow at some time in their lives. Most growth occurs in most organisms in the first parts of their lives. After a period of time, all living things stop growing.

The range of growth of each living thing depends on what kind of organism it is. People usually reach a height of about five to six feet. Oak trees grow to a certain size within a range. Some plants that live on the tops of mountains never get more than an inch or two high.

What conditions in the environment of a mountaintop would influence plant size?

Responding to the Environment

The environment is all the things around you. Your house, your school, the sky, the sun, the soil, and many organisms are all parts of your environment. Your environment includes everything you can see, hear, or feel around you.

The environment of an organism is very important to it. People can live on Earth because the environment is right. There is enough oxygen. The temperature is not too hot or too cold. There is food and water. All organisms need certain things in their environment. And all organisms respond to the things in their environment.

To **respond** means to act in return or in answer to something. A mouth-watering piece of apple pie will make you respond. You will reach for the pie. A vicious dog will also make you respond. You will stay away from it. A plant will respond to dry soil by drying out and eventually dying. A cat will respond to a flea on its back by scratching.

Living things need a balanced environment. Ecologists devote a lot of their study to keeping a balanced environment.

Name five things in your school environment that make you respond.

All Living Things Are Made of Cells

Cells are the basic building blocks of life. They are tiny units of living material. Every living thing is made of cells. Most living bodies are made of many cells stuck together. You are made of about 60 trillion cells. A few kinds of organisms consist of only one cell. Most cells are too small to be seen without a microscope.

You will learn much more about cells later. The important thing to remember now is that if something is not made of cells, it is not alive.

The Final Word on Living: Dying

There is one more thing that all living things must do: die. Different organisms have different life spans. That is, they live for different lengths of time. People live for about 75 years. A housefly lives for only a few days.

When organisms die, they are **recycled**. That means that their bodies are used again by nature.

Think of a forest floor. Dead animals and dead plants **decay** there. That means they break down into smaller pieces. The decayed organism gets mixed in with the soil. There are important nutrients in all living things. The nutrients in the dead organisms help to feed plants growing in the soil. Other animals may eat these new plants. In this way, all living things are recycled.

Housefly	Hamster	Worker	Dog	Rabbit	Horse	Elephant	Human	Clam	Giant
17–29	3	Bee	14–15	18	30	65	75	100	tortoise
days	years	6 years	years	years	years	years	years	years	130
									years

Each kind of organism has a different life span.

Chapter Review

Chapter Summary

- All living things are called organisms. There are many very different kinds of organisms on Earth. But they all share six characteristics:

  1. All organisms can move on their own. Animals fly, swim, walk, run, or crawl. Plants move much more slowly than animals, but they also move.

  2. All organisms reproduce. This means that they give birth to offspring, or new organisms.

  3. All organisms use energy. As they grow, move, breathe, and work, energy is burned. Living things must take in food to get the energy they need.

  4. All organisms grow. Different kinds of plants and animals grow to different sizes. Once they reach that size, they stop growing.

  5. All organisms respond to their environment. That means they act in return or in answer to the things around them.

  6. All living things are made of cells. Cells are tiny units of living material.

- When organisms die, they are recycled. That means their bodies break down and become nutrients for other living things.

Chapter Quiz

Write the answers to these questions on a separate sheet of paper.

1. Name five kinds of organisms that live in your town or city.

2. Name ten non-living things that can be found in your town or city.

3. Give an example of a way that a plant moves on its own.

4. What are offspring?

5. When you are sitting still, what kind of work is your body doing?

6. Write at least three sentences to describe the environment you are in right now.

7. What are the building blocks of which all living things are made?

8. How long does a housefly usually live?

9. What happens to the bodies of organisms after they die?

10. Name the six characteristics of life.

Moving Organisms

Match each kind of organism with the main way that it moves. Write a letter next to each number on a separate sheet of paper.

1._____ rabbit   a. walks

2._____ bird   b. hops

3._____ human   c. flies

4._____ worm   d. slides

Mad Scientist Challenge: Earth's Environment

Scientists think that life may exist on other planets. But so far there is no proof of this. On a separate sheet of paper, list the ways in which the Earth's environment makes the Earth a good place for life to exist.

Chapter 3

The
Biology
Lab

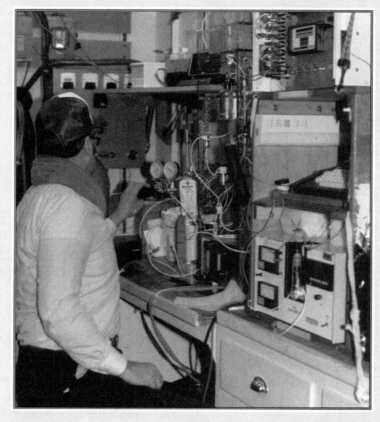

This scientist is studying the chemicals in ocean water. Why is the laboratory so important to science? Why is so much work done there?

Chapter Learning Objectives

- Define scientific measurement.
- Name the tools of biology.
- Describe how to run safe lab experiments.

Words to Know

area   the number of square units that a surface covers

centimeter   1/100th of a meter

kilometer   one thousand meters

lens   a curved glass used in microscopes

magnify   to make something appear larger

measurement   the size, quantity, or amount found by measuring

meter   the standard unit of length in the metric system, equal to 39.4 inches, or slightly more than 3-1/4 feet

metric units   the standard units of measurement in the metric system, based on the number ten and multiples of ten

millimeter   1/1000th of a meter

specimen   something that is looked at under a microscope

unit   a fixed amount or quantity that is used as a standard of measurement

volume   the amount of space an object occupies

In 1818, a woman named Mary Shelley wrote a book that has since become famous. The book is about a young biologist named Frankenstein. In her story, the biologist worked long, hard hours in his lab. He wanted to learn the secret of life.

Frankenstein pieced together the parts of dead bodies. Finally, he brought a creature to life. But Frankenstein's creation was an eight-foot monster. Eventually the monster destroyed the biologist.

Scientists use laboratory equipment to test their ideas.

This is just a story. But there are scientists working in labs all over the world. Could the Frankenstein story really happen?

Probably not. But a lot of amazing things *do* happen in biology labs. Biologists have discovered cures for diseases. They have found ways to make food richer in nutrients. They have discovered ways to grow bigger flowers in the garden.

In this chapter you will learn about some important lab skills. You will learn how to use a microscope. You will learn how to measure amounts. Also, you will learn about safety in the lab.

What Is a Biology Lab?

Scientists use experiments to test their ideas. Experiments are carried out in labs. A lab can be just about any place. Sometimes a lab is an entire forest. A biologist might study the birds in a stand of birch trees. Usually a lab is a special room or set of rooms. These rooms are equipped with the tools of science. The picture on the left shows some important tools of biology.

Measurement and Lab Work

Measurement is a way of finding out the amount of something. Measurement is a part of every biologist's work. If there is nothing to measure, there cannot be an experiment.

For example, take the question, "Do you like the color red?" There is no way to measure this question. The answer is simply your feelings. But you could ask, "How many people in the world like the color red?" That is a question that has an answer because the number of people can be counted. Here is another question. "How far can you hit a baseball?" The answer to this question can be measured in an experiment.

Anything that cannot be measured remains a theory. Take, for example, the question, "How many stars are there in the Milky Way?" Scientists can make smart guesses. But they do not have a way to make an exact count. Some time in the future, however, a scientist may come up with a way to make an exact measurement. Then the scientist will be able to prove the theory with experiments.

Think about the experiments with the car in Chapter 1. There were many measurements, including speed, distance, and gas mileage.

Biology Practice

Read each of these questions. On a separate sheet of paper, write the ones that can be answered scientifically.

How much do you love me?

How tall am I?

Are tall people or short people better looking?

How far is it to the shore?

The Metric System of Measurement

Most people in this country measure length in inches, feet, and yards. We measure distances in miles. Inches, feet, yards, and miles are all **units** of measurement. A unit is a fixed amount or quantity used by everyone when measuring.

Most people in the world use **metric units** to measure things. All scientists use metric units. Meters and kilometers are metric measurements of length. A liter is a metric measurement of volume. Perhaps you have bought soft drinks in liter-size bottles.

The metric system is based on the number ten and multiples of ten. It is much like our money system.

Metric Units of Length

The main metric unit of length is the **meter**. You may know about meters from watching sports on TV. Many running events are measured in meters.

A meter is equal to 39.4 inches. This is just 3.4 inches longer than a yard. Most full-grown people are about 1-1/2 to 2 meters tall.

You know from money that "cent" means one out of a hundred. A **centimeter** is 1/100 of a meter. One inch equals about 2-1/2 centimeters. "Milli" means one out of a thousand. A **millimeter** is 1/1000 of a meter.

A **kilometer** is one thousand meters. This is a little more than half a mile.

Metric Units of Area and Volume

Area is the number of square units that a surface covers. The area of this page is 440.4 square centimeters. The area of the Earth is 510,100,000 square kilometers.

Volume is the amount of space an object takes up. Biologists use volume to measure liquids, such as blood or lake water. The main metric unit for measuring volume is the liter. This is a little bigger than a quart. Biologists sometimes must measure tiny amounts of a liquid. Then they use milliliters. A milliliter is 1/1000 of a liter.

What Is a Microscope?

A microscope is a device for looking at things too tiny to see with the naked eye. The simplest microscope is a magnifying glass. To **magnify** means to make something look bigger.

A magnifying glass is made with a **lens**. This is a curved piece of glass. It makes the object beneath it appear bigger to someone looking through it.

The microscope in the picture below has two lenses. One is called the *objective*. The other is called the *eyepiece*. These two lenses working together magnify more than a single lens.

Using a Microscope

Anything that a biologist looks at under a microscope is called a **specimen**. Specimens are placed on slides. A *slide* is a piece of glass. The specimen goes on top of the slide. A cover slip is placed on top of the specimen to hold it in place.

The specimen, between the two pieces of glass, is then slipped onto the microscope's *stage*. Two clips hold the slide in place.

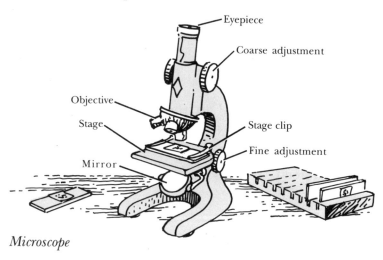

Microscope

A biologist looks through the eyepiece to study a specimen. There are two knobs for focusing a microscope. One is for *coarse*, or major, adjustments. The other is for fine tuning.

People in Biology: Anton van Leeuwenhoek

In 1660, a Dutch scientist named Anton van Leeuwenhoek used a magnifying lens to study tiny things. He discovered tiny living things that other scientists didn't know even existed.

Leeuwenhoek set out to improve the magnifying lens. He built the first microscope, and then another. He built 250 microscopes in his lifetime. Even the best of his devices were quite simple. They made things look about 200 times bigger than they were.

Today, high-powered microscopes can make things look 250,000 times bigger than they are! Scientists can study the tiniest parts of organisms.

Safety in the Biology Lab

Safety is an important part of biology lab experiments. Working with fire and some chemicals can be very dangerous. Here are a few important safety rules that should *always* be followed.

1. Read every word in the instructions for an experiment before beginning. Before you start, be sure to have all the materials and equipment you need.

2. Keep a very clean work area. Clear the area of everything except the things you need for the experiment. Tell your teacher about any spills immediately.

3. Never taste or touch any substances in the lab unless instructed by your teacher or book to do so. Do not eat or drink or chew gum in the lab. Keep your hands away from your face.

4. Always make sure your equipment is in good working order. Never use frayed cords or containers with chipped glass.

5. Whenever you are instructed to wear eye goggles, do so.

6. Know the exact location of clean, running water. This is important if you should accidentally get a substance in your eye or an open cut.

7. Always tell your teacher if even the tiniest fire is started by an experiment. Know where the fire extinguisher is. Have your teacher show you how to use it.

8. Always tie back long hair. Make sure loose clothing is tucked in or buttoned up. This is to make sure no clothing or hair gets in a substance or fire.

9. Wash your hands with soap and water after working in the lab.

10. Follow all instructions exactly. If you don't understand something, ask your teacher.

Only when you follow an exact procedure do you get meaningful results in your experiments.

Chapter Review

Chapter Summary

- Biologists test their ideas with experiments. Anywhere an experiment is carried out is called a lab. This can be a whole meadow or one small room.

- Measurement is a way of finding out the amount of something. Measurement is a part of every biologist's lab work. If there is nothing to measure, there cannot be an experiment.

- All scientists use the metric system of measurement. This system is based on the number ten and multiples of ten. The meter is the standard metric unit of length. The liter is the standard metric unit of volume.

- The microscope is an important tool of biology. It lets scientists look at things too small to see with the naked eye. One or two lenses are used to magnify specimens (make them look bigger).

- Safety in the lab is very important. Always read all the instructions before beginning an experiment.

Chapter Quiz

Write the answers to the following questions on a separate sheet of paper.

1. Suppose a biologist wants to study a plant that lives only on mountaintops. Where would that biologist set up a lab?

2. Suppose you wanted to know what is the most popular kind of music: rock, country and western, or blues. Can you find out by running a scientific experiment? If yes, how would you do it? If no, why not?

3. What is the main metric unit of length? How many inches is it equal to?

4. What is area?

5. What is volume? What is the main metric unit of volume?

6. Suppose a biologist wants to know the length of an earthworm. Which metric units would he or she use?

7. Why are microscopes helpful to biologists?

Fill in the Blank

Fill in the missing word so that each sentence is true. Write your sentences on a separate sheet of paper.

1. Biologists carry out their experiments in _____.

2. When you look through a _____, things appear bigger than they really are.

3. In metric units, it is several thousand _____ from the west coast of the United States to the east coast.

Mad Scientist Challenge: Frankenstein

Do you think the Frankenstein story could happen in real life? Why or why not? Explain your answer on a separate sheet of paper.

Unit 1 Review

Answer the following questions on a separate sheet of paper.

1. List the five steps in the scientific method.

2. What field of biology studies the characteristics of offspring?

3. What are the six characteristics all living things share?

4. Where do animals get energy?

5. What is a response?

6. What happens to the dead organisms on a forest floor?

7. What is a measurement?

8. Why do you need running water in the lab?

9. Why does a microscope have two lenses?

10. Why must you follow an exact procedure in the lab?

Life and the Cell

Unit 2

Chapter 4

Cells: The Building Blocks of Life

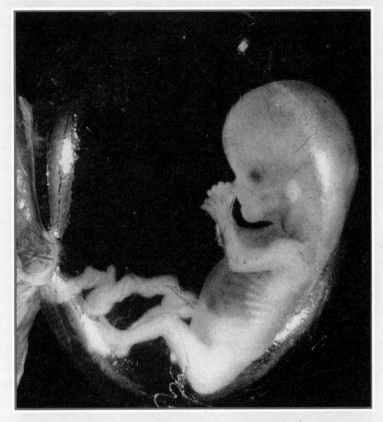

You began life as a single cell. Then you developed into an extremely complex organism. This is a photograph of a 13-week-old fetus.

Chapter Learning Objectives

- Name the elements of life.
- List the parts of a cell.
- Explain how plant cells differ from animal cells.
- Describe the structure of organisms.
- Explain the process by which cells reproduce.

Words to Know

atom   the smallest particle of matter

cell membrane   a thin protective covering around a cell

cell wall   a hard covering around plant cells

chloroplasts   the parts in a plant cell that store sunlight to make food

chromosomes   the parts of a cell that pass on the characteristics of living things to offspring

cytoplasm   a jellylike substance filling a cell

elements   the basic substances of which all matter is made

mitochondria   structures in a cell that convert food into energy

mitosis   the process of cell reproduction

molecule   two or more atoms joined together

nucleus   (plural, nuclei) the part of a cell that controls all the other parts

organ   a group of tissues working together, such as a heart or kidney

system   a group of organs working together

tissue   a group of cells that all do the same job

vacuoles   openings in a cell that store food, water, or wastes

You began life as a single cell. That single cell already had all the six characteristics of life. When you were born nine months later, that single cell had become an organism of 2 trillion cells. When your body stops growing, it will have about 100 trillion cells.

What exactly are these cells of which you are built? In this chapter you will learn what cells are made of. You will also learn about several important parts of the cell.

The Elements of Life

Everything in the universe is made of *matter*. Matter is anything that takes up space. Scientists know of more than one hundred distinct types of matter. Each kind of matter is called an **element**. Oxygen, carbon, hydrogen, helium, and uranium are all elements. Rocks, air, water, clothing, cars, plants, animals, and people are all made of elements.

Each kind of element can be broken down into tiny particles. The tiniest particle of an element is called an **atom**. Often, atoms join together. Two or more atoms joined together are called a **molecule**. For example, a water molecule is made of two hydrogen atoms and one oxygen atom. Everything in the universe is made of molecules.

In this book, we are only concerned with *living* matter. All living matter is made of cells. There are six main kinds of elements found in the cells of organisms. They are shown in the chart on the next page. These elements combine in your cells to form different chemicals your body needs.

The Elements in Living Matter	
Element	**Percent**
Oxygen	65
Carbon	18
Hydrogen	10
Nitrogen	3
Calcium	2
Phosphorus	1
Trace elements	1

Cells Are the Machines of Life

Think of your body as a life factory. Your cells are the machines that do all the work. They produce energy. They make new skin when you need it. They carry messages from your brain to the rest of your body. Your cells carry out all the work of your body.

Some creatures are made up of only one cell. Yet these tiny organisms can carry out all the life functions: moving, reproducing, using energy, growing, and responding to their environment.

Most of the organisms that you know about are many-celled. Billions of cells act together to do the work of the body.

Discovery of the Cell

In 1665, over three hundred years ago, a man named Robert Hooke was looking at different things under his microscope. He cut a very thin piece of cork. Cork is part of the bark of a certain kind of oak tree. He looked at the cork under his microscope.

Hooke saw many tiny openings in the cork. They looked to him like the small rooms used by monks. These small rooms are usually called cells. So Hooke named the tiny openings in cork *cells*. The name has lasted.

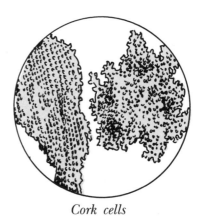

Cork cells

The Parts of a Cell

What Robert Hooke saw were really *dead* cells. Today, with the help of high-powered microscopes, biologists can study *living* cells very closely. There are many parts to cells. You will learn about a few of them.

- **Cell Membrane**

Around the outside of each cell is a **cell membrane**. This is a thin, elastic covering. The cell membrane has several important jobs. It holds the cell together. It also protects the cell. It keeps harmful substances from entering. At the same time, the membrane lets good things, like food and oxygen, pass into the cell. It also allows waste products to be passed out of the cell.

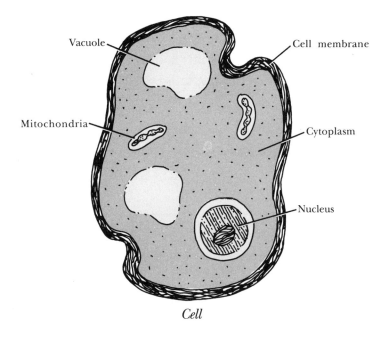

Cell

• Nucleus

Inside each cell is a tiny nucleus. The **nucleus** acts as the cell's brain. Special chemicals in the nucleus direct everything that happens in the cell. The nucleus is held together by another membrane.

Inside the nucleus are special structures called **chromosomes**. These are thread-shaped. They store information about an organism's characteristics. For example, your chromosomes store information about your sex, the color of your hair, your height, and many, many other things. You will learn a lot more about chromosomes later.

• Cytoplasm

Cytoplasm is a jellylike substance within the cell. The nucleus and all the other structures in the cell float in the cytoplasm. This substance is mostly water.

Chromosomes are made of a chemical called DNA. Chromosomes pass the characteristics of a living thing on to its offspring.

- **Mitochondria**

Mitochondria act as the cell's power plant or battery. They take food and break it down to make energy. Mitochondria are plump, sausage-shaped structures.

- **Vacuoles**

Vacuoles are the storerooms of cells. They are open areas. Food, wastes, and water can be stored in the vacuoles.

Biology Practice

Write the answers to these questions on a separate sheet of paper.

1. Name two of the main elements in your body.
2. Which part of a cell controls the others?
3. Which part of a cell stores wastes?
4. Who discovered cells?

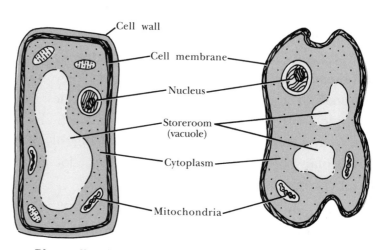

Plant cell

Animal cell

How Plant Cells Are Different from Animal Cells

Both plant cells and animal cells have all the parts described above. But plant cells are different from animal cells in several important ways.

First, plant cells have special structures called **chloroplasts**. These structures help plants make food from sunlight. Animals cannot make their own food like plants can. You will learn much more about this food-making process later.

Plant cells usually have fewer vacuoles than animal cells. But the one or two they do have are very large. Plant cells need these large storerooms to keep water.

There is a third important difference between plant and animal cells. Plant cells have a **cell wall** around their membranes. This cell wall is hard and protects the cell.

Specialized Cells

You are a very complicated organism. There are many different kinds of cells doing work in your body. They all have the same basic parts. But each kind of cell is also set up to do a certain job.

Remember the idea that your body is like a factory. The cells are the machines that do the work. Skin cells have the job of covering your body. So they are flat. Muscle cells help you move. So they are long and can stretch. Nerve cells deliver messages all over your body. They are long and stringy, like telephone wire.

Your blood has two different kinds of cells: red blood cells and white blood cells. There are many fewer white blood cells. But they have a very special job.

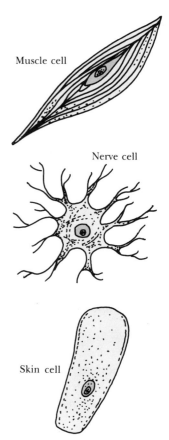

Muscle cell

Nerve cell

Skin cell

White blood cells destroy harmful things that invade your body, such as certain bacteria. The membranes of white blood cells form pockets around the bacteria. In this way, they kill the invaders.

When you are sick, your body makes many more white blood cells than usual. These cells rush to the scene of your illness like an ambulance. They help to clean up your body.

Building Organisms from Cells

All the different cells in your body are organized into groups. Groups of cells that work together doing the same job are called **tissues**. Blood cells work together to make blood tissue. Muscle cells work together to make muscle tissue. Nerve cells work together to make nerve tissue.

Groups of tissues sometimes work together to make up an **organ**. Your heart, lungs, brain, stomach, and eyes are all organs. For example, muscle tissue makes your heart pump. Nerve tissue tells it *when* to pump. Connective tissue holds the parts together. Blood tissue delivers food and oxygen to and from the heart. So several tissues work together to make up your heart.

Finally, organs work together to make body **systems**. Your digestive system is made up of your mouth, stomach, intestines, and several other organs. Your circulatory system is made up of your heart, veins, arteries, and other organs.

You will learn much more about the tissues, organs, and systems of your body. For now, just remember how your body is organized.

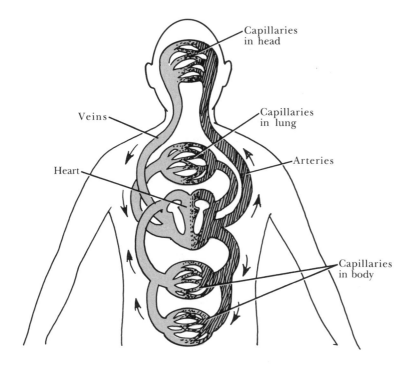

Circulatory system

Plants also have tissues, organs, and systems. Flowers, leaves, stems, and roots are all plant organs. Each is made of a special kind of tissue. Plant organs work together to make systems.

Cell Reproduction

When you cut yourself, the cut heals over. How does this happen? Your cells reproduce. New cells take over the jobs of the damaged or dead ones.

Your body cells are reproducing all the time. Cells die, just like organisms. New cells must replace the old ones.

Cells reproduce by dividing in two. This process is called **mitosis**. The two new cells are called daughter cells. There are several important steps in mitosis:

1. First, the chromosomes in the nucleus of the parent cell make exact copies of themselves. This is so the daughter cells will each get the same number of chromosomes as the parent. Remember that chromosomes are the structures that determine an organism's characteristics. Chromosomes duplicate the qualities of the parent cell in the offspring.

2. Next, the membrane around the nucleus of the parent cell disappears. The two sets of chromosomes spread out into the cytoplasm. One set goes to one end of the cell. The other set goes to the other end.

3. Then the middle of the cell pinches together. The parent cell breaks up into two daughter cells. The cell membrane separates and seals each of the daughter cells.

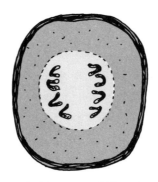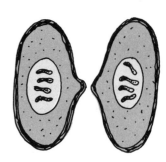

The stages of mitosis

Daughter cells are exactly like the parent cell. This is because the daughter cells are made with exact copies of the parent's chromosomes. Therefore, a muscle cell will only reproduce other muscle cells. The same is true for a blood cell, a nerve cell, or any other kind of cell. It can only reproduce more of its own kind.

On the Cutting Edge

Sometimes abnormal cells form in an organism. These abnormal cells are called *cancer* cells. Cancer cells reproduce much more quickly than healthy cells. After a while, they can block healthy functions of the body.

Biologists are working hard to understand cancer. They do know *some* of the causes. For example, smoking can cause lung cancer. Some support a theory that the electromagnetic fields from power lines and power stations are contributing to an increase in cancer.

Scientists have found some good treatments for cancer. But they do not yet know how to cure cancer completely. Perhaps in your lifetime scientists will discover a cure for cancer.

Chapter Review

Chapter Summary

- Everything in the world is made of matter.

- Matter is made of elements. Scientists know of more than one hundred elements.

- The tiniest particle possible is called an atom. Two or more atoms joined together make up a molecule.

- The six main kinds of elements found in living matter are oxygen, carbon, hydrogen, nitrogen, calcium, and phosphorus.

- All living matter is made up of cells. The outside of a cell is covered with a membrane. The nucleus acts as the cell's brain. Chromosomes, found in the nucleus, store information about an organism's characteristics. The cell's cytoplasm is a jellylike substance in which all the other parts float. The mitochondria are the structures that make energy for the cell. The vacuoles are the cell's storerooms.

- Plant cells differ from animal cells in three important ways.

- A group of cells that do the same job is called tissue. A group of tissues that work together to do a job is called an organ. A group of organs that work together to do a job is called a system.

- Cells reproduce by dividing in two. This process is called mitosis.

Chapter Quiz

Write the answers to the following questions on a separate sheet of paper.

1. What are the six main elements in your body?
2. What is the main difference between living matter and non-living matter?
3. Name two different jobs your "cell machines" do for your body.
4. What holds a cell together? Describe this part.
5. What structures in cells make energy? Describe these structures.
6. What part of the cell directs everything that happens in the cell?
7. Why do plants need large vacuoles?
8. What do chloroplasts in plant cells do?
9. What is another word for a group of muscle cells that all work together?
10. Why are daughter cells exactly like the parent cell?

Systems of Your Body

On a separate sheet of paper, name one organ in each of the following systems:

Digestive system

Circulatory system

Nervous system

Mad Scientist Challenge: Reporting on Biology

On a separate sheet of paper, write a report. Call your report "The Three Differences Between Plant and Animal Cells." Describe each of the three differences.

Chapter 5

Energy and Cells

Some dolphins can swim as fast as twenty-five miles per hour. Where do they get all that energy?

Chapter Learning Objectives

- Explain how organisms get energy from food.
- Describe how plants make their own food.
- Explain the difference between respiration and breathing.
- Compare respiration and photosynthesis.

Words to Know

chlorophyll a green substance within the chloroplasts in plant cells that traps sunlight

complex carbohydrates foods such as whole grains, potatoes, and pasta, that provide the body with slow-burning energy

photosynthesis the process by which plant cells make food from sunlight, water, and carbon dioxide

respiration the process by which cells get energy from food and oxygen

semi-permeable having tiny pores so that certain molecules can pass through

Consider these facts. A certain bird, the spine-tailed swift, can fly up to 106 miles per hour. The cheetah, the fastest-moving land animal, can run 65 miles an hour. The red kangaroo can jump over things as high as 10 feet. It can jump forward 30 feet. Hummingbirds can beat their wings 90 times a second.

The question is, how do these animals get the energy to do such amazing things? Where does a plant get the energy to grow? How do you get the energy to get out of bed every day? To get to school? To do all the things you do?

The answer is that your cells make energy from food and oxygen. In this chapter you will learn how they do this.

Remember that energy is the ability to do work. When a cheetah runs or a kangaroo jumps, it is doing work.

What Is Energy?

The universe is made up of two things: matter and energy. You know that matter is anything that takes up space. Most of the time you can see and feel matter.

But energy is not matter. It does not take up space. Yet you know it is there. There is energy in a flowing river. There is energy in the shining sun. A tree uses energy to grow. You use energy every time you take a breath. Any time something moves, it uses energy. Biologists define energy as the ability to do work.

All Living Things Get Their Energy from Food

If you are like most creatures, you like to eat. All living things get their energy from food. The world's largest living land animal is the African elephant. In the wild, it eats 770 pounds of plants a day. It drinks 40 gallons of water. How does it make use of all this food and water?

Energy can be stored in matter. For example, a match stores energy. When it is struck, the energy is released as light and warmth.

In a similar way, food stores energy. The cells in an organism do the work of getting energy from food. But how can 770 pounds of food and 40 gallons of water get inside a cell?

How Substances Enter and Leave Cells

Cells need food, water, and oxygen. They must dispose of carbon dioxide and other wastes. How do these things get in and out of the cell?

The cell membrane is **semi-permeable**. That means there are tiny pores, or holes, in the cell membrane. Certain kinds of molecules can pass into the cell through the cell membrane. And certain kinds of molecules can pass out of the cell through the cell membrane.

So food must be broken down into tiny molecules before it can enter cells. Suppose you eat a plate of spaghetti. Your digestive organs break the spaghetti down. This takes several hours. But after a while, the spaghetti is nothing but molecules of food. These molecules are now small enough to pass through the membranes of your body cells. Then your cells go to work making energy.

Many of the systems in your body work together to supply food to your cells.

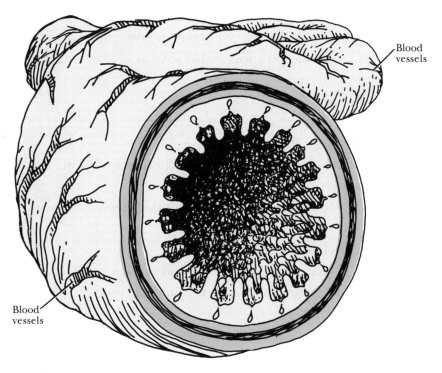

Blood vessels

Blood vessels

Small intestine

Respiration: The Way Cells Make Energy

Two things are needed for cells to make energy: food and oxygen. While you are eating that plate of spaghetti, you are also breathing. Breathing lets you get oxygen out of the air. These oxygen molecules pass into your cells through the cell membranes.

The mitochondria in your cells are the structures that make energy. The food and oxygen molecules combine in the mitochondria. When they do, energy is released. This process is called **respiration**. It is the most important thing that your cells do.

There are two waste products of respiration: carbon dioxide and water. Carbon dioxide is a gas. It, along with the water, passes out of your cells.

food + oxygen = energy + carbon dioxide + water

Some people confuse breathing and respiration. Breathing is the way you take air into your lungs and let it out. Respiration is the way the mitochondria in your cells use oxygen and food to make energy.

Mitochondria are the plump, sausage-shaped structures that act as power plants in your cells.

Biology Practice

Write the answers to the following questions on a separate sheet of paper.

1. How is it possible for certain molecules to pass into or out of your cells?
2. What is respiration?
3. What do your cells need to make energy?
4. What are the waste products of respiration?

Biology Alert

Athletes are always concerned about energy. What they eat can make the difference between winning and losing.

Biologists have found that a certain kind of food gives the most energy. Grains, such as rice and wheat, noodles, breads, and potatoes, are all high-energy foods.

These foods are called **complex carbohydrates**. They break down slowly in the body. They give an athlete energy for a long period of time. Fruits and vegetables are also good sources of carbohydrates.

Simple carbohydrates are found in candy, soft drinks, and other sweets. These are not good for athletes. This kind of carbohydrate burns very quickly in the body. The athlete may get a quick rush of energy. But then he or she will feel a big drop in energy. Complex carbohydrates are the best energy foods for athletes.

Photosynthesis: How Plant Cells Make Food

Respiration explains how both plants and animals get energy. But how do plants get food in the first place? You certainly have never seen a plant eating a meal.

You, like other animals, eat plants and other animals for food. Plants get their food in a different way. Plants make their own food using energy from sunlight, carbon dioxide, and water. This process is called **photosynthesis**.

Remember that plant cells have special parts that animal cells do not have. These parts are called chloroplasts. Chloroplasts contain a green coloring called **chlorophyll.** Chlorophyll is very good at absorbing energy from the sun. Its green color traps the sunlight.

Carbon dioxide passes into plant cells right from the air. Water also passes through cell membranes in the cells of plant roots. The carbon dioxide and water meet in plant cells.

The sun energy, trapped by chlorophyll, causes the water and carbon dioxide molecules to combine. They form a new substance: simple sugar. This simple sugar is food for the plant.

Photosynthesis also produces some oxygen. This passes out of plant cells as a waste.

Respiration needs oxygen to produce carbon dioxide and water. Photosynthesis needs carbon dioxide and water to produce oxygen.

energy + carbon dioxide + water = food + oxygen

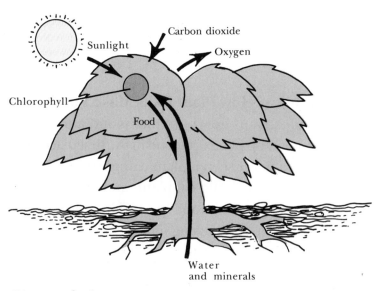

Photosynthesis

Once plant cells have made their own food, they carry out respiration just like animal cells. Mitochondria break down the sugars. This releases energy.

The Life Cycle of Food and Energy

Look again at what happens in respiration:

food + oxygen = energy + carbon dioxide + water

Compare that with what happens in photosynthesis:

energy + carbon dioxide + water = food + oxygen

Do you notice something about these two processes? They are the exact opposite of each other. Respiration uses food and oxygen to make energy, carbon dioxide, and water. Photosynthesis uses energy, carbon dioxide, and water to make food and oxygen.

This is one of the most important cycles for all living things. Energy from the sun sets the cycle in action. Without the sun, there could be no life on Earth. Without plants making food, animals would have nothing to eat.

The cycle of respiration and photosynthesis means plants and animals need each other to survive.

Chapter Review

Chapter Summary

- The universe is made up of two things: matter and energy. Matter is anything that takes up space. Energy is the ability to do work.

- All living things get energy from food.

- Cell membranes are semi-permeable. This allows food and oxygen molecules to enter cells. Food and oxygen combine in the cell's mitochondria. This releases energy. This process is called respiration.

- Plant cells are able to make their own food. They do this by a process called photosynthesis. First chlorophyll, a green coloring in chloroplasts, traps energy from the sun. This energy causes water and carbon dioxide molecules to combine to form sugar.

- Plants carry out respiration to get energy from the sugar.

- Respiration and photosynthesis are opposite processes.

  In respiration:

  food + oxygen = energy + carbon dioxide + water

  In photosynthesis:

  energy + carbon dioxide + water = food + oxygen

  This is one of the most important cycles for all living things.

Chapter Quiz

Write answers to the following questions on a separate sheet of paper.

1. How do you know that energy is not matter?
2. From what source of energy do all plants make food?
3. Why can food, oxygen, and water enter and leave cells?
4. What structures in the cell make energy from food?
5. Write the formula for respiration.
6. How is respiration different from breathing?
7. Why are complex carbohydrates better than simple carbohydrates for athletes?
8. Write the formula for photosynthesis.
9. What is meant by the life cycle of food and energy?
10. An animal can live in the dark for a long time. A plant cannot. Explain why this is true.

Talking About Biology

On a separate sheet of paper, describe the respiration/photosynthesis cycle. What sets the cycle in motion? Why would animals not be able to eat if plants did not carry out photosynthesis?

Mad Scientist Challenge: Carbohydrates

In a notebook, keep track of what you eat for a week. Be especially accurate about carbohydrates. Write down the days you ate simple carbohydrates, such as candy and soft drinks. Write down the days you ate complex carbohydrates, such as whole grain cereal, rice, or potatoes. Write down how you felt each day. Then, compare your notes. Which foods gave you more energy? What conclusions can you draw from this?

Chapter 6

Genetics and the Secret Code of Life

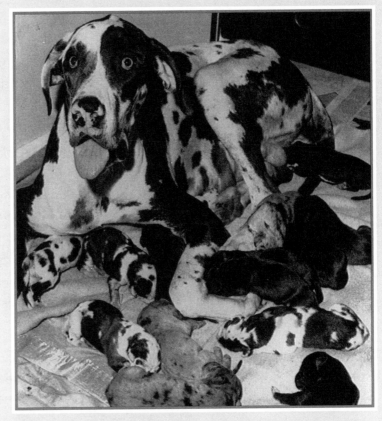

Why don't all these offspring look exactly like their mother? Why don't you look exactly like your parents? What determines your characteristics?

Chapter Learning Objectives
- Describe how the study of genetics began.
- Define genes and DNA.
- Describe how DNA molecules create a code that determines your characteristics.

Words to Know

asexual reproduction the process of one cell splitting to form two daughter cells

DNA molecules in the nuclei of cells that make up chromosomes and serve as a "code" for an organism's traits

dominant traits traits that are stronger in an organism's genetic code and more likely to appear in offspring

egg the female sex cell

genes the parts of the DNA molecule that control the development of specific traits

heredity the process by which traits are passed from parents to offspring

mutation a change in the genetic code, causing an abnormality in the organism

recessive traits traits that are weaker in an organism's genetic code and less likely to appear in offspring

sexual reproduction the joining of two sex cells, a sperm and an egg, to produce offspring

sperm a male sex cell

traits characteristics, which may be inherited, that identify organisms as individuals

Every cell in your body holds a secret code. The code is exactly the same in each cell. It is a set of instructions. These instructions give the color of your hair, eyes, and skin. They tell what your shape and size is. They say whether you have normal vision or not. These instructions hold information about many aspects of you. In this chapter you will learn how each cell in your body holds a secret code for you.

What Is Genetics?

All living things reproduce. Their young are called *offspring.* Parents pass many of their own **traits** to their offspring. Traits are characteristics, such as size, shape, and color.

The passing of traits to offspring is called **heredity**. And the study of heredity is called *genetics.*

How the Study of Genetics Began

Genetics is a new and exciting field of biology. People have been studying genetics for only about 100 years. Important breakthroughs are made each year.

The study of genetics began with an Austrian monk. His name was Gregor Johann Mendel. He grew 22 different kinds of pea plants. Some were short and bushy. Others were tall and climbing. Some had white flowers, others pink flowers. Some produced round seeds, and others wrinkled seeds.

Mendel crossbred the pea plants. That means that he had different kinds of pea plants reproduce together. He crossbred tall plants with short plants. He crossbred white-flowered plants with pink-flowered plants. He crossbred round-seeded plants with wrinkle-seeded plants.

Gregor Mendel

What Became of Mendel's Experiments?

Mendel got some interesting results from his experiments. When he crossed tall and short plants he always got tall plants. When he crossed pink-flowered and white-flowered plants, he always got pink-flowered plants. When he crossed round-seeded plants with wrinkle-seeded plants, he always got round seeds.

Mendel had discovered that a trait from one parent may mask, or hide, the trait from the other. He found that certain traits were stronger than others. In pea plants, tallness was a stronger trait than shortness. Pink flowers were a stronger trait than white flowers. And round seeds were stronger than wrinkled ones.

The traits that are more likely to appear in an organism are called **dominant traits**. The masked traits are called **recessive traits**.

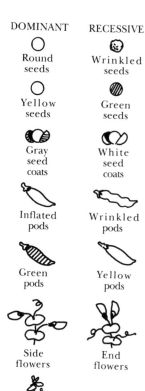

DOMINANT	RECESSIVE
Round seeds	Wrinkled seeds
Yellow seeds	Green seeds
Gray seed coats	White seed coats
Inflated pods	Wrinkled pods
Green pods	Yellow pods
Side flowers	End flowers
Long stems	Short stems

Biology Alert

Skin color is a human trait. Why do people have different colors of skin? A chemical called *melanin* causes skin to be dark. All people have some melanin in their make-up. Freckles are caused by melanin. Dark-skinned people have more melanin than others. A few people lack melanin altogether. They are said to be *albino*.

DNA: The Secret Code of Life

Since Mendel's time, biologists have learned much more about traits. They have found that an organism's traits are determined by a code. This code is found in the chromosomes of the organism's cells. Remember

DNA molecule

that chromosomes are thread-like structures found in the cell nuclei.

Chromosomes are made of molecules called **DNA**. A DNA molecule is shaped like a spiral staircase. DNA is one of the largest molecules found in living things. Each cell contains many such molecules.

The DNA molecule is really made of thousands of molecules linked together. The exact order of these smaller molecules forms a life code. This code controls all the activities in the cell. If the order of the molecules gets changed, the code will be changed.

In a way, DNA molecules are like tiny computers. They store huge amounts of information and instructions. Every cell in your body uses these instructions.

Biology Practice
Write answers to the following questions on a separate sheet of paper.
1. Who began the study of genetics?
2. What is a dominant trait?
3. What are chromosomes made of?

Name some of your own traits. Include hair color, eye color, skin color, height, shape, and eyesight.

What Are Genes?
Genes are certain sections of the DNA molecules. Genes come in pairs. Half come from the mother, and half from the father. Each gene contains specific genetic information. It is the combination of genes that determines specific traits.

For example, it is a combination of certain genes that determines what color hair you have. Another combination of genes determines whether you will be tall or short. All of these combinations of genes are contained in the DNA molecule. That is why the DNA molecule is so complex. You may have as many as 10,000 genes in each cell. The genes in every cell in your body are exactly like the genes in every other cell.

Mendel used the word "traits." He didn't know that traits were controlled by genes. Offspring get a set of genes from each parent. Some genes are recessive. Some are dominant. Recessive traits may only appear when the offspring gets a recessive gene from each parent.

The DNA code is a little like a telephone number. If you change one digit in the number, you will not get the same person. If you change one gene, you may get a different characteristic.

It takes a combination of genes from both parents to determine each trait.

On the Cutting Edge

Biologists have learned how to cut specific genes out of DNA molecules. They can put a gene from one organism into the DNA molecule of another organism. This process is called *gene-splicing*.

By gene-splicing, biologists have created a kind of bacterium that "eats" oil. This bacterium may be used in oil spills in the ocean. Another kind of bacterium has been created that produces an important medicine for people with diabetes.

Scientists are also experimenting with *gene therapy*. In 1990, a four-year-old girl became the first person to receive human-gene therapy. The girl had a rare disease in which she was born without a special gene needed to keep her healthy. The doctors were able to add the needed gene to her white blood cells.

People in Biology: Maria Nieto

Maria Nieto is a scientist working to find out how white blood cells deal with harmful viruses and bacteria. Remember that white blood cells keep you healthy. They kill other cells that are not supposed to be in the body.

Nieto studies the genes that tell the white blood cells what to do. How does a white blood cell know what viruses and bacteria are? How does it know to kill them? Nieto hopes to answer these questions in her research.

Mutations: Breaks in the Genetic Code

Once in a while, something will go wrong with the genetic code. A bobcat may give birth to a kitten with no claws. Or a wolf may give birth to a pup with no sense of smell.

For some reason, the gene combinations in the DNA were set up slightly differently. This causes the code to change. The offspring are born with an abnormality called a **mutation**.

Most mutations are harmful and cause the offspring to die. Bobcats without claws cannot climb trees or protect themselves. Wolves that cannot smell cannot find food.

However, once in a while, a mutation is helpful. If it is, the organism will live and pass the mutation along to offspring. The mutation becomes part of the offspring's genetic code.

Can you think of a mutation that might help a human being? What human trait or traits do you think could be improved?

Asexual and Sexual Reproduction

Each kind of organism has a certain number of chromosomes in its cells. Cats have 32 chromosomes (or 16 pairs). Dogs have 78 (39 pairs). Carrots have 18 (9 pairs). People have 46 (23 pairs).

You have read how cells reproduce. They make exact copies of their nuclei (including the chromosomes). Then they split in half. When this happens, the daughter cells are exactly alike. This is called **asexual reproduction**.

However, the offspring of most plants and animals are not exactly like the parents. This is because they reproduce by **sexual reproduction**. In sexual reproduction, two cells *join*, one from each parent, to make the offspring. Organisms that reproduce sexually have special cells to do this.

The male sex cells are called **sperm**. The female sex cells are called **eggs**. Sex cells have only half the chromosomes that other cells do. In human sex cells, there are only 23 chromosomes instead of the usual 46.

There is a good reason for this. In sexual reproduction, the sperm and egg cells join. If they both had the full number of chromosomes, the offspring would have twice the usual number. Instead, each parent gives only half of its chromosomes. That way the offspring has the full number.

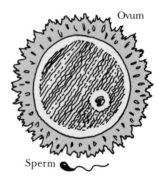

Sperm

Sperm cell and egg cell

In sexual reproduction, the offspring are always somewhat different from the parents. This is because the offspring receive half their chromosomes from each parent. Each offspring will get a special combination of genes. This combination will make him or her unique.

On the Cutting Edge

There are two kinds of twins: fraternal and identical. *Fraternal twins* are born when the mother produces two separate eggs. Both eggs are fertilized by sperm.

Identical twins form from one egg. Early on inside the mother, that one egg splits into two. The two babies have almost exact genes. For this reason, identical twins are often studied by geneticists. They study what is alike about them. They look at what is different. In that way, they can know more about what is controlled by genes and what is not.

Identical twins

Plant and Animal Breeding

Genetics may be new as a science. But people have been using the ideas of genetics for a long time. Plants and animals have been bred to get the best products for thousands of years.

Today, scientists breed oranges without seeds. They breed cattle without horns. They have bred chickens that lay eggs almost every day. The study of genetics can be very useful to people.

Environment and Traits

The genetic code does not control everything about you. Your environment also plays a big part in your traits.

An apple tree may have genes to bear lots of sweet fruit. But the tree may live during a long dry season. It may be planted in poor soil. Its environment may not allow the tree to bear any fruit at all.

The same is true for people. Perhaps a person has genes for being very tall. But that person may eat very poorly. He may not get any exercise. Then he will not grow as tall as he could have grown.

The environment may even influence the genetic code. Organisms with unfavorable traits may not survive to have offspring.

Biology Alert

Scientists have long debated the effects of heredity and environment. Some scientists believe that inherited traits are more important. Some scientists believe that the environment is more important. They argue about which one is the greater influence on an organism's development. This debate is at the heart of the study of genetics.

Chapter Review

Chapter Summary

- Genetics is the study of how traits are passed from parents to offspring. This study began about 100 years ago when a man named Gregor Johann Mendel crossbred pea plants. He discovered that certain dominant traits masked recessive traits.

- Biologists now know that traits are controlled by molecules called DNA. These molecules make up the chromosomes in cell nuclei. Certain parts of DNA molecules are called genes. It is the combination of genes that determines different traits in an organism.

- Sometimes a mistake occurs in the reproduction of chromosomes. The combinations of genes in the DNA get mixed up. This changes the genetic code. This is called a mutation. Most mutations are harmful to organisms.

- In asexual reproduction, a cell splits in two. The daughter cells are exactly like the parent cell.

- In sexual reproduction, two sex cells join to form a new cell. Male sex cells are called sperm. Female sex cells are called eggs. With sexual reproduction, the offspring are always different from the parents. That is because the offspring receives some genes from each parent.

- The ideas of genetics have been used for many years. Plants and animals are bred to get better products.

- Genetics does not control everything about an organism. The environment also plays a big role in developing characteristics.

Chapter Quiz

Write the answers to the following questions on a separate sheet of paper.

1. Do any two people ever have the same genetic makeup? If yes, who?
2. What did Mendel discover with his experiments?
3. What kind of molecule holds the code of your life? Where are these molecules found?
4. What are genes?
5. What causes differences in skin color among people?
6. What are female sex cells called? What are male sex cells called?
7. Why are offspring born of asexual reproduction exactly like the parents?
8. Why are offspring born of sexual reproduction different from the parents?

Fill in the Blank

Complete the following sentences on a separate sheet of paper.

1. Each section of a DNA molecule that stands for a trait is called a _____.
2. Chromosomes are found in the _____ of a cell.
3. In sexual reproduction, a _____ cell and an _____ cell join to form a new cell.

Mad Scientist Challenge: Heredity

On a separate sheet of paper, write down the color of your parents' eyes. Are they the same? Are your eyes the same color as theirs? Are your parents' eyes different? If so, do you have your mother's eyes, or your father's? What does this tell you about heredity?

Chapter 7

Simple Organisms

There is a world of life all around us we never see. Microscopic one-celled organisms fill the air we breathe and the water we drink. These are one-celled algae, magnified 62,000 times.

Chapter Learning Objectives

- List the characteristics of the moneran, protist, and fungus kingdoms.
- Describe the problem of classifying viruses.
- Explain the importance of blue-green algae.

Words to Know

algae (singular, alga) plant-like protists

bacteria (singular, bacterium) simple one-celled organisms in the moneran kingdom

cilia tiny hairs some protists use to move

classification the system biologists use to group organisms by type

flagella a long tail some one-celled organisms use to move

food chain a grouping of organisms in which lower organisms are eaten by higher ones

fungi (singular, fungus) organisms that have no chlorophyll, yet cannot move about like animals in search of food. Mushrooms, molds, and yeasts are *fungi.*

monera (singular, moneran) tiny organisms that have some nucleic materials, but no true nuclei, in their cells

protists tiny one-celled organisms that are neither plants nor animals but that often have characteristics of both

protozoans animal-like protists

pseudopods a kind of arm amebas use to move

spores reproductive cells of organisms such as ferns, fungi, and algae

virus a microscopic structure made of DNA and a coating of protein. Viruses are dependent on living cells to reproduce.

When people use makeup, they may be smearing tiny creatures on their faces. That's because a kind of one-celled organism is sometimes used in producing skin creams. Other one-celled organisms are used in making bread, beer, cheese, and pickles.

These forms of life are too tiny to see. That's why you are not usually aware of them. Yet one-celled organisms live all over your body. They live all over the walls of your home. They float around in the air you breathe. The organisms you will learn about in this chapter are neither plants nor animals. Most of them are single-celled.

Grouping Organisms into Kingdoms

You have already learned what elephants and palm trees have in common. They share the six characteristics of life. But they still have many differences. Elephants are a part of the animal kingdom. Palm trees are a part of the plant kingdom.

Organisms in the animal kingdom must search for food. Animal cells do not contain chlorophyll. Organisms in the plant kingdom use chlorophyll to make their own food. Plants are not able to walk, fly, or swim in search of food.

Biologists group organisms into kingdoms. This grouping is called **classification**. Living things are grouped by the structures of their bodies. For a long time biologists classified living things into only two kingdoms: plant and animal. Today, they use five kingdoms: moneran, protist, fungus, plant, and animal. In this chapter you will learn about the moneran, protist, and fungus kingdoms. These three kingdoms are made up of the simplest forms of life.

Before you learn about the three new kingdoms, review what you know about the plant and animal kingdoms. Name three important differences between plant and animal cells.

THE FIVE KINGDOMS		
Kingdom	**Description**	**Examples**
1. Moneran	Single-celled Has no cell nucleus	Bacteria Blue-green algae
2. Protist	Most are single-celled Has a nuclei	Protozoans Algae
3. Fungus	Many-celled Cannot move Has no chlorophyll Has cell walls	Yeasts Molds Mushrooms Mildew
4. Plant	Many specialized cells Uses chlorophyll and sunlight to make food Has cell walls	Seed plants Ferns Mosses
5. Animal	Has no chlorophyll Many specialized cells Eats other organisms Cannot make its own food	Insects Mammals Birds Fish

The Moneran Kingdom

Monera are tiny, one-celled organisms. You cannot see them with the naked eye. But monera are the most numerous organisms on Earth. They live everywhere—in the sea, on mountaintops, in the desert, in the Arctic, and in hot springs. Biologists believe monera are the oldest form of life on Earth.

There are about 3,100 kinds of monera. The two main groups are **bacteria** and *blue-green algae.*

There is an important reason why bacteria and blue-green algae have their own kingdom. The cells of these organisms do not have nuclei. They also lack many other structures found in most cells. They *do* have DNA. But they have only a single chromosome.

Most of these tiny organisms are harmless. There are many living on your skin and inside your body right now. However, many bacteria cause problems. Bacteria cause tooth decay. They can also spoil food. And some bacteria cause infection and disease.

The Importance of Blue-Green Algae

Blue-green algae are in the moneran kingdom. The cells of these algae contain chlorophyll. So they are able to make their own food by photosynthesis.

Blue-green algae are extremely important to other living things. They begin many **food chains**. A food chain is a grouping of organisms in which lower organisms are eaten by higher ones. Energy is transferred from one organism to the one that eats it. For example:

BLUE-GREEN ALGAE are eaten by MINNOWS which are eaten by TROUT which are eaten by HUMANS.

There are many more examples of food chains beginning with blue-green algae. Without these tiny monera, many animals would not have food.

Blue-green algae contribute something else that's necessary to life: oxygen. Remember that oxygen is a waste product of photosynthesis. Blue-green algae are tiny organisms. But there are billions and billions of them on Earth. As they carry out photosynthesis, they release a huge amount of oxygen.

If blue-green algae have chlorophyll, why aren't they plants? Because they do not have nuclei in their cells.

The atmosphere of the early Earth had little or no oxygen. Many biologists believe that blue-green algae released much of the first oxygen into the atmosphere. When enough oxygen was present, more complex organisms were able to develop. They could gain their energy by respiration.

Biology Alert

Many species of blue-green algae grow well in polluted water—too well. You may have seen a pond or lake covered with green slime. The slime is really a huge amount of blue-green algae. This is called an *algal bloom*.

Algal blooms use up a great deal of oxygen in the water. This, in turn, kills fish. Biologists are trying to clean up polluted waters to prevent algal blooms.

Bacteria

Bacteria are another kind of moneran. They are also very tiny. They have cell walls, like plants. But they do not have chlorophyll. And bacterium cells do not have nuclei.

Bacteria are very helpful to people in many ways. They are used to make cucumbers into pickles. They are also used to make cabbage into sauerkraut. Milk becomes cheese because of the action of bacteria.

Bacteria feed off dead matter. This includes leaves, dead animals, and the food you eat. Bacteria break dead matter down into molecules. This is how dead plants and animals are returned to the soil of the Earth. If it weren't for bacteria, the Earth would be covered with dead waste.

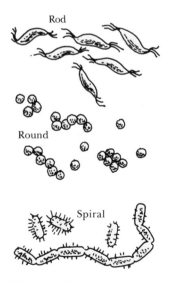

Shapes of bacteria

Bacteria are helpful to plants, too. In fact, plants would not be able to live without the help of bacteria. All plants need nitrogen. But they are not able to use the nitrogen in the air. They need the nitrogen to be changed into another form called *nitrates*. Bacteria do this job. They change nitrogen from the air into nitrates in the soil.

When gardeners make compost heaps, they are using bacteria to help them grow their plants. The gardeners dump all their organic waste (matter that is or once was alive) on the compost pile. This waste can include egg shells, vegetables, bread, and coffee grounds.

Then bacteria go to work on this dead organic matter. They break it down. In doing so, they help form nitrates. The compost heap becomes rich fertilizer for the garden. When the gardener spreads the decayed "garbage" on the garden plot, the plants flourish.

Some bacteria are harmful. They can cause food poisoning. This is why people refrigerate food. Bacteria do not like very cold places. And bacteria also dislike very hot places. That is one reason why we cook our food.

Amazing Biology

Freeze-drying is another way to protect food from bacteria. Freeze-dried foods were first developed for astronauts in space. Perhaps you have taken freeze-dried foods on camping trips. First these foods are prepared fresh. Then all the water is removed from the food. Next the food is put in packages that completely block out moisture and oxygen. Bacteria need moisture and oxygen to live.

Freeze-dried foods can be stored for very long times without refrigeration. To eat them, a person simply opens the package and adds water.

The Protist Kingdom

Protists are another group of one-celled organisms. They are not monera because they have nuclei in their cells. Yet they are neither plants nor animals. In a way, the protist kingdom is a catch-all kingdom. It is made up of organisms that do not clearly fit into any other kingdom.

Here's an example. One kind of protist, the *euglena*, can move around like an animal. It has a long tail that it whips back and forth. This tail is called a **flagella**. The flagella pushes the organism forward. The euglena can hunt and eat food like an animal. Yet the euglena has chlorophyll. Like a plant, it carries out photosynthesis for some of its food.

There are two main groups of protists: **protozoans** and **algae**. Protozoans are more like animals than plants. Algae are more like plants than animals. There are several thousand species of each.

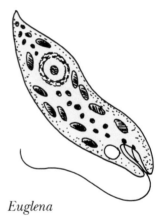

Euglena

Protist algae are different than blue-green algae in the moneran kingdom. Blue-green algae do not have cell nuclei, though they have DNA. Protist algae do have nuclei in their cells.

Protozoans: Animal-like Protists

Protozoans eat bacteria, algae, other protozoans, and organic matter.

There are three main ways protozoans move. One type of protozoan, an *ameba*, moves by using its **pseudopods**. The ameba is like a glob of jelly. It moves its pseudopods forward and slides along. The ameba catches its food by encircling it with two pseudopods. This makes a vacuole. Then the ameba digests the food.

Other protozoans, such as the *paramecium*, move by means of **cilia**. These are thousands of tiny hairs on the organism. As these hairs beat like tiny oars, the organism moves forward.

Some protozoans move by means of a flagella.

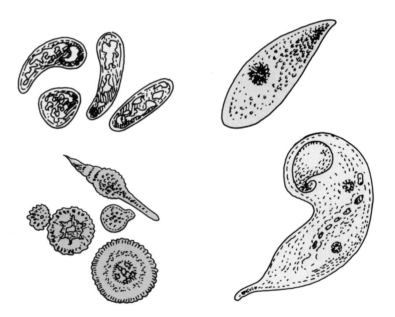

Protozoans

Algae: Plant-like Protists

Almost all algal protists contain chlorophyll. They carry out photosynthesis for food. Algae live in water or in very wet land areas. They all have nuclei in their cells.

The euglena, an algal protist, has an eye spot. This spot is sensitive to light. So the eye spot helps lead the euglena to the light it needs for photosynthesis.

Some algal protists are many-celled. But they are not considered plants because all their cells do the same work. In other words, they do not have specialized cells.

Algae are extremely important to life on Earth. They take part in many food chains. They also produce most of the oxygen on Earth.

Biology Practice

On a separate sheet of paper, answer the following questions.

1. How do scientists group living things?
2. Why are bacteria important to the Earth?
3. What is a flagella?
4. Why are biologists trying to clean up polluted waters?

The Fungus Kingdom

You have probably eaten mushrooms in salad or on pizza. Mushrooms are part of the fungus kingdom. **Fungi** are not plants. They do not have chlorophyll in their cells. Nor are they animals. They cannot move around to hunt for food. Their cells have nuclei, so they cannot be monera. And they are too big to be protists. So fungi have a kingdom of their own.

There are several kinds of fungi. These include *mildews, molds, yeasts,* and *mushrooms.* All fungi have hairy structures. These are easy to see on bread or fruit mold. The hairy structures on mushrooms are often underground.

Like bacteria, fungi eat dead organic matter. They do this by using a special chemical. The chemical breaks down the food into molecules. Then the fungi absorbs the food molecules. Fungi eat wood, clothing, leather, and other dead organisms. Athlete's foot is a kind of fungi that feeds on the dead skin on people's feet. Most fungi live in moist, dark places.

Fungi reproduce by means of **spores**. Spores are special reproductive cells in round cases called *spore cases*. When the spore cases break open, the cells are released. If the cells land somewhere that is wet and warm enough, new fungi will grow.

Kinds of Fungi

Mildew is a fungus that grows in particularly damp places. It often grows on bathroom tiles around the bathtub or shower.

Yeast is another kind of fungi. It is used in making bread and beer. The yeast cells eat the sugar molecules in bread dough. Then they carry out respiration. In respiration a gas, carbon dioxide, is released. These bubbles of gas push the bread up. This is how baking bread "rises." Carbon dioxide also makes the bubbles in beer.

Molds like dark warm places. Perhaps you have found mold on old bread or fruit.

Mushrooms are also fungi. There are many kinds of mushrooms. Never eat any you find in the out-of-doors. Many poisonous fungi look just like the kind you find in grocery stores. One bite of some kinds of mushrooms can be deadly.

How Are Viruses Classified?

This is a book about life. Should **viruses** be included? Biologists do not agree about whether viruses are living things or not.

Viruses are structures with an outer coat of protein. Inside this coat is a core of DNA. Only living things contain DNA, the code of life.

Viruses cause the common cold, warts, measles, mumps, influenza, polio, and AIDS. They do this by invading cells. Once inside a cell, the virus takes over the cell's machinery. It uses the cell to reproduce itself. When doing this, the virus acts just like a living thing.

Yet by themselves, viruses show no signs of life. Without a host cell, they cannot reproduce. They look like dry crystals. Viruses have been described as genes in search of a cell.

You may now understand why biologists are confused about viruses. Are viruses living things that sometimes don't act like it? Or are they non-living things that sometimes act as if they are alive?

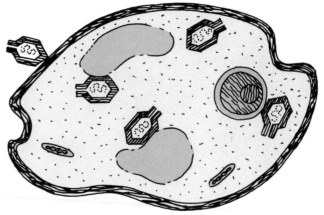

Viruses

Biology Alert

AIDS is a deadly disease caused by a virus. So far there is no known cure for AIDS. Biologists are trying to find a way to stop it from spreading.

For now, the best way to prevent AIDS is to understand the facts about the disease. The AIDS virus cannot be gotten by casual contact. Shaking hands or touching someone with AIDS will not infect another person. Mosquitoes cannot carry the AIDS virus. It does not travel through air, either.

There are four ways to get the AIDS virus: 1) through sexual contact with someone who has the virus; 2) by sharing hypodermic needles with someone who has the virus; 3) from a blood transfusion in which the blood has been contaminated by the virus; or 4) from a mother who passes the virus on to her unborn child.

Chapter Review

Chapter Summary

- Biologists classify organisms into five kingdoms: plant, animal, moneran, protist, and fungus.

- Monera are one-celled organisms without nuclei in their cells. They live just about everywhere on Earth. The two main groups of monera are bacteria and blue-green algae.

- Bacteria feed off dead matter. They help break down all the organic waste on Earth.

- Blue-green algae carry out photosynthesis to feed themselves. In doing so, they produce huge amounts of oxygen for the Earth.

- Protists are one-celled organisms that are neither plants nor animals. They have nuclei in their cells. The euglena carries out photosynthesis like a plant and looks for food like an animal. Protozoans are animal-like protists. They move by pseudopods, cilia, or flagella. Algae are plant-like protists. They are very important in many food chains.

- The fungus kingdom is made up of mushrooms, molds, yeasts, and mildews. These organisms do not carry out photosynthesis. Yet they do not go out and look for food, either. They feed on dead organic matter. Fungi reproduce by spores. Most fungi like dark, warm places.

- Viruses may or may not be alive. They are made up of DNA with an outer coating of protein. By themselves, they cannot function. By invading living cells, however, they can reproduce. Viruses cause many diseases including AIDS, mumps, the common cold, polio, and influenza.

Chapter Quiz

Write answers to the following questions on a separate sheet of paper.

1. What are the five kingdoms called?
2. What is different about the moneran kingdom?
3. Name three ways bacteria are helpful to people.
4. Name two ways bacteria can be harmful to people.
5. Why is the euglena a protist rather than a plant or animal?
6. What are the three ways protozoans can move?
7. What kind of organism do some people smear on their faces?
8. Describe a spore.
9. Why do people refrigerate and cook food?
10. What is a virus?

Naming the Kingdoms

On a separate sheet of paper, write the kingdom in which each of the following organisms belong.

1. protozoan
2. daisy
3. euglena
4. blue-green algae
5. beetle
6. ameba
7. mold
8. bacteria
9. human being
10. yeast
11. palm tree
12. mildew

Mad Scientist Challenge: Viruses

Do you think viruses are living or non-living? On a separate sheet of paper, write a short report. First write a sentence stating your position. Then write at least two sentences supporting your position.

Answer the following questions on a separate sheet of paper.

1. How are plant cells different from animal cells?

2. Why do you have specialized cells?

3. What do white blood cells do?

4. What are tissues?

5. What are organs?

6. What is mitosis?

7. What part of the cell makes energy?

8. What are dominant and recessive traits?

9. What is a mutation?

10. Describe the ways that protozoans move.

Plants: The Food Makers

Chapter 8

The Study of Plants

Some branches of banyan trees grow straight down. There they take root in the ground and grow into trunks.

Chapter Learning Objectives
- Name the five important characteristics of plants.
- Describe what plants need in order to grow.
- List two reasons why plants are important.

Have you ever considered a job working with plants? If you are strong, you might find work as a logger. If you are artistic, you might get a job arranging flowers for flower shops.

Farmers work with plants every day. Other plant lovers work as gardeners in parks. Designing landscapes is another good job.

For any of these jobs, you must understand plants. In this chapter, you will learn the general characteristics of plants. Why are they important? What defines a plant?

How Important Are Plants?

Chocolate comes from a bean grown on a plant. Your favorite pair of blue jeans was made from a plant. Plants may even keep your house warm. If you use a fireplace, you burn wood. Coal and gas are plant products, too. Several important drugs for curing diseases come from plants.

Every single thing you eat is a product of plants. That even includes steak or bacon. After all, if plants weren't carrying out photosynthesis to make food, cows and pigs would have nothing to eat. Without cows and pigs, there would be no steak or bacon.

Finally, plants give you the oxygen you need to breathe and carry out respiration. Remember that oxygen is a waste product of photosynthesis. If green plants did not give off oxygen, you would not be reading this book. You would not exist at all.

Plants are the starting point of the food chain. Without plants, there would be no food for any animals to eat.

What Is a Plant?

You know that biologists group all organisms into kingdoms. You have already studied three kingdoms of life: the moneran kingdom, the protist kingdom, and the fungus kingdom.

So what is a plant? That may sound like a silly question. Everyone knows that plants are trees, bushes, grasses, and flowers. But plants have a few special characteristics. These characteristics put them in the plant kingdom.

1. Plants have chlorophyll in their cells. All plants make their own food by using energy from the sun.

2. Plants are many-celled. Even if they have chlorophyll in their cells, one-celled organisms cannot be plants.

3. Plants have specialized cells. This means that each plant organism has several different kinds of cells. The different cells perform different jobs. Like animals, plants have tissues, organs, and systems.

4. The cells of plants have cell walls.

5. Plants cannot move from place to place. That is to say, they cannot walk, swim, or fly. Plants *do* move. But they stay rooted in the ground.

Plants carry out photosynthesis and respiration. They need specialized cells to make sure all of their parts get everything they need.

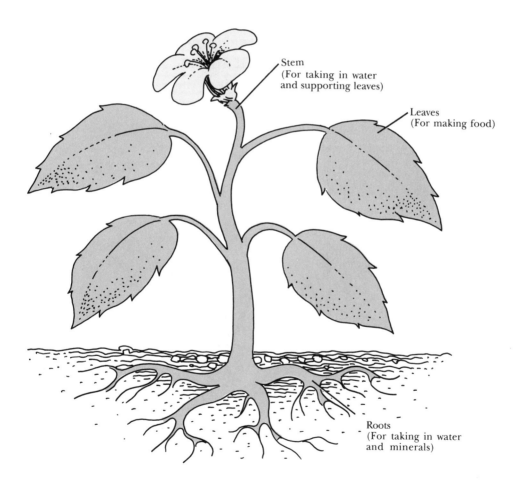

Stem
(For taking in water and supporting leaves)

Leaves
(For making food)

Roots
(For taking in water and minerals)

What Plants Need to Grow

Like all living things, plants need food, oxygen, and water. They also need light, carbon dioxide, and minerals.

Plants need carbon dioxide for photosynthesis. They need oxygen for respiration. They get both of these gases from the air.

Plants also need light for photosynthesis. They get light from the sun. And plants get water, which is also needed for photosynthesis, from the ground.

You have already learned how plants get food. They make their own. The chlorophyll in plant cells traps sunlight. Carbon dioxide from the air enters plant cells. Water is absorbed from the ground. The energy from the sunlight combines the carbon dioxide and water. The result is sugar.

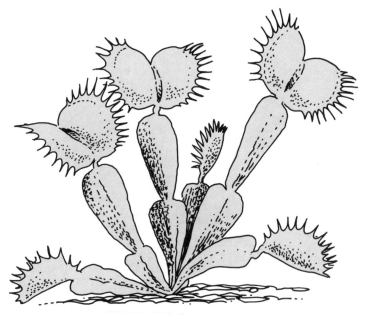

Venus flytrap

Biology Practice

Plants need food, oxygen, water, light, carbon dioxide, and minerals. On a separate sheet of paper make a chart with two headings: "Plant Needs" and "Source." List everything a plant needs to grow. Then identify the source of each of these needs.

Plant Needs	Source

Amazing Biology

Have you ever heard of a meat-eating plant? Some plants grow in soil that doesn't have all the nutrients they need. So these plants capture insects for extra nutrients.

The pitcher plant has leaf parts that are shaped like pitchers. It traps and digests insects in these leaf parts.

The Venus flytrap catches insects on its leaves. The leaves open wide to lure an insect. The leaves have a sticky, sweet substance that acts as bait for the insect. When the insect lands on the leaf, it is stuck. The leaf closes like a trap around the insect.

These plants have very specialized cells for catching and eating bugs. But they are still plants. They are rooted to the ground. And they get most of their food by photosynthesis.

Plants Grow in Soil

Soil is the top layer of Earth's surface. It is made up of rocks, minerals, water, air, and decayed plant and animal matter. Almost all plants must grow in soil. The soil gives the plants important minerals and other nutrients.

Big particles in soil are called sand. If a soil is too sandy, the water will run through it too quickly. The smallest particles in soil are called clay. Clay holds water. If a soil has too much clay, the water will not drain fast enough. Many plants will rot if they sit in wet ground for too long.

Humus is the organic matter in soil. This is dead plants and animals that have been broken down by bacteria. Humus provides very important nutrients. The best soil for most plants has a good mixture of sand, clay, and humus. This kind of soil is called **loam**.

While most plants grow well in loam, not all do. Desert plants, for example, grow very well in dry, sandy soil. Some plants, such as moss, can only grow where there is a constant source of water.

The nutrients in the soil may determine what plants will grow there. Different plants need different nutrients.

Most farm crops grow very well in loam.

On the Cutting Edge

Besides providing oxygen for animals, trees do a number of other amazing things.

One of the most promising new cancer drugs is taxol. This is made from the bark of the Pacific yew tree. About six 100-year-old Pacific yew trees are needed to produce enough taxol to treat one patient for a year. In the past, the yews were considered weeds by loggers and were burned. In March 1991, the U.S. Forest Service ordered an end to burning yew trees.

The neem is another amazing tree. Indians have understood and used its special properties for hundreds of years. Only recently have scientists begun to understand the tropical evergreen. Chemicals from the neem tree may kill several disease-causing agents, including the fungus of athlete's foot and ringworm. Brushing one's teeth with neem twigs deters gum disease. The neem's seeds help to kill off harmful insects. This tree has so many healthful uses, it is sometimes called "the village pharmacy."

Chapter Review

Chapter Summary

- Plants are very important to our lives because they provide food, clothing, shelter, and fuel. Not only do we eat plants directly, but we eat animals that eat plants. Plants begin many food chains. Also, plants provide oxygen for people and other animals to use in respiration.

- There are five important characteristics of plants: 1) Plants have chlorophyll in their cells. 2) Plants are many-celled. 3) Plants have specialized cells. 4) The cells of plants have cell walls. 5) Plants cannot move from place to place.

- To grow, plants need food, oxygen, and water. They also need light, carbon dioxide, and minerals. The light comes from the sun. The food comes from photosynthesis. The oxygen and carbon dioxide come from the air. The water and minerals come from the soil.

- Almost all plants must grow in soil. Soil is made up of rocks, minerals, water, air, and decayed plant and animal matter. For most plants, the best soil is a mixture of sand, clay, and humus.

Chapter Quiz

Write the answers to the following questions on a separate sheet of paper.

1. Name five different kinds of jobs that involve working with plants.
2. Name five kinds of plants that you eat.
3. What plant products can be used as fuel?
4. Where does most of the oxygen in the air come from?
5. Why is plant photosynthesis important to you?
6. What two gases do plants need in order to grow?
7. What do plants get from soil?
8. What makes up soil?
9. What is the organic matter in soil called?
10. A mixture of what three things makes good soil for most plants?

Characteristics of Plants

On a separate sheet of paper, list the five characteristics of plants.

Mad Scientist Challenge: Understanding Plants

Visit a nursery. Pick out a plant that you like. Write its name on the top of a sheet of paper. Ask a person working at the nursery for information about the plant. Then write answers to the following questions.

1. What kind of soil does the plant like?
2. Does it grow best in sun, shade, or half and half?
3. How much water does the plant need?
4. How often should it be fertilized?

Chapter 9

Classes of Plants

Notice how small this man looks next to a giant redwood. How do nutrients reach the top of such a tall tree?

Chapter Learning Objectives
- Describe the difference between vascular and nonvascular plants.
- List the main ways that plants are classified.
- List two characteristics of mosses and ferns.

Words to Know

fertilization   the joining of egg and sperm cells

frond   the leaf of a fern

germination   the process by which an embryo develops and finally breaks out of the seed

nonvascular plants   plants that do not have structures for transporting water

plant embryo   the early, undeveloped stage of a new plant

vascular plants   plants that have structures for transporting water

The plant kingdom is huge. It includes a great deal of variety, from tiny mosses all the way up to huge redwoods. Biologists group plants in order to study them. In this chapter you will learn how biologists classify plants.

Transport Cells

The plant kingdom has two main groups. One group has special cells for transporting water, food, and minerals. These cells connect to form tube-like structures. Roots absorb water. Then the water is moved up these tube-like structures to other parts of the plants.

At the same time, plant leaves make food. Some of this food can be moved down the tube-like structures to feed the roots. Plants that have these structures for transporting water and food are called **vascular plants**. Plants that do not have these special transport cells are called **nonvascular plants**. Water cannot be stored or moved in nonvascular plants.

Vascular plants have a circulatory system, like animals do. Nonvascular plants do not have a circulatory system.

Mosses and liverworts

You often find moss at the base of a shady tree. The moss keeps the soil moist and protects the roots.

Nonvascular Plants: Mosses and Liverworts

Nonvascular plants must live in places that have a constant supply of water. These plants are usually very small. *Mosses* and *liverworts* are two kinds of nonvascular plants. These are the simplest plants on land. Biologists believe that mosses were the first plants to grow on land.

You may be familiar with mosses. These green plants often form soft carpets on forest floors. Sometimes they grow on logs or on wet rocks. Mosses like wet, shady places. Shade keeps moisture from evaporating.

Mosses are very important in nature. They are among the first plants to grow in barren areas. They grow rapidly, and form a great deal of humus. This humus makes the soil more suitable for more complex plants.

Mosses do not have true roots or leaves. Root-like structures on mosses cannot deliver water to the rest of the plant. And the leaf-like structures are really just sheets of cells.

But mosses are different from algae because their cells are specialized. All algae cells do the same work. In mosses, though, the root-like parts are better at soaking up water than the leaf-like parts. Also, these root-like parts are underground. Only the leaf-like structures carry out photosynthesis.

Liverworts also grow in wet places. They can be found along stream banks or near springs. A liverwort looks like a leathery leaf lying flat against the ground. It has hair-like structures that anchor the plant to the ground. These hair-like structures also absorb water from the soil.

Simple Vascular Plants: Ferns

Ferns are simple vascular plants. They have specialized cells for transporting food and water. They also have true roots, stems, and leaves. Ferns grow in woods, swamps, and gardens where there is lots of water. Some grow several feet high.

The stems of ferns are underground. These grow horizontally just beneath the soil surface. The leaves of a fern are called **fronds**. They grow up from the stem. The roots grow down from the stem.

Amazing Biology

Millions of years ago giant fern forests covered the Earth. The land in those days was wet and marshy. The climate was warmer than it is now. Tree ferns, 30 feet high, were common. The greenery then was much thicker than it is today.

This greenery of millions of years ago provides fuel for today—coal. Here's how the coal formed.

As the giant ferns died, they fell to the ground. They decayed. Eventually, they became covered with soil. The soil pressed down on the plant matter. More ferns died and more soil packed down. Over millions of years, the compressed plants became coal.

This coal is still deep in the Earth today. Coal miners go underground to dig it up. Then the coal is burned for energy.

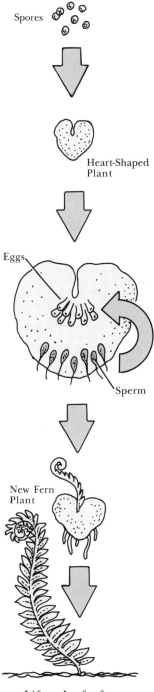

Spores

Heart-Shaped Plant

Eggs

Sperm

New Fern Plant

Life cycle of a fern

Fern Reproduction

Ferns have an interesting way of reproducing. It happens in two stages. On the bottom of fern leaves, you will see little brown spots. These are spore cases. When these open, spores fly out. If a spore lands in a good place for growing, a small plant grows. This small plant does not look like the parent fern, however. It is a small, heart-shaped plant.

Then the second stage in fern reproduction begins. The heart-shaped plant forms sperm and egg cells. The sperm cells swim to the egg cells through dew or rainwater on the plant.

The joining of sperm and egg cells is called **fertilization**. A new fern plant grows from the fertilized egg.

The first stage in fern reproduction is *asexual*. There is only one parent cell, the spore. The second stage is sexual. There are two parent cells, the sperm and the egg.

The word "fertilization" applies to all organisms. Any time a sperm and an egg cell join, it is called fertilization.

Biology Practice

Write the answers to the following questions on a separate sheet of paper.

1. What are transport cells?
2. What is a liverwort?
3. Where do mosses grow?
4. How are mosses different from algae?

The Seed Plants

Ferns are a simple kind of vascular plant. Seed plants are more complex vascular plants. Most of the plants you know are seed plants.

The plant kingdom is divided into nonvascular and vascular plants. Then the vascular plants are divided into two groups: ferns and seed plants.

All farm plants, grasses, flowers, and evergreen trees are seed plants. Most of the plants you eat are seed plants. Wheat, rice, peas, beans, broccoli, apples, and oranges all come from seed plants. Seed plants reproduce by seed instead of by spore.

What Is a Seed?

A seed is a protective covering for the first stage of a tiny new plant. The tiny new plant inside the seed is called a **plant embryo**. Most of the seed consists of a food supply for the embryo. The embryo must have this food because it may stay in its covering for months or even years. The food allows the embryo to live until conditions are right for it to grow into a full plant.

To grow, seeds must have warmth and water. Most plants produce many more seeds than they need. This is because most seeds dry out and die.

The tiny beginning of any organism is called an embryo. Even an unborn human baby is called an embryo. You will read this word many more times in your study of biology.

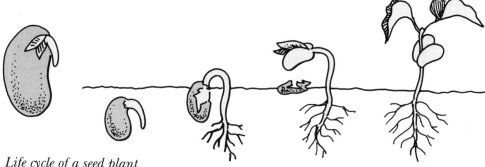

Life cycle of a seed plant

The Success of Seed Plants

Seed plants have many advantages over other kinds of plants. They are able to live in harsher environments. There are several reasons for their success.

First, they have well-developed vascular tissue. This means they are very good at transporting water. Think of redwood trees. These trees are hundreds of feet high. Yet they can transport water from the ground up to the top branches!

Seed plants can exist in very dry places. They can send roots deep in the soil to reach water. Unlike ferns, they do not need water for fertilization. In seed plants, the sperm cell is carried to the egg cell by wind, insects, or animals.

The seed itself is the greatest advantage of seed plants. A seed has a protective coat that is stronger than a spore case. This coat holds in moisture. Also, the embryo inside the seed has a store of food. The embryo can last a long time before dying—sometimes even years. This improves its chances of arriving in a place where it can grow. Spores, on the other hand, have just one chance. They have little protection and no food store.

A seed becomes a plant by a process called **germination**. When a seed germinates, the embryo inside it starts developing and growing. To do this, the seed needs the right temperature and moisture. And it needs enough oxygen. Special chemicals in the seed tell it when it is time to germinate.

Cones and Flowers

The seed plants are divided into two groups: *cone-bearing plants* and *flowering plants*. Cone-bearing plants are usually evergreen trees. Pines, firs, redwoods, and spruces are all cone-bearers. Most of these trees have needles for leaves. The seeds of these plants are found in the cones.

Flowering plants produce seeds inside a fruit. Daisies, grass, corn, lemon trees, and maple trees are all flowering plants. You will read more about cone-bearing and flowering plants in the next two chapters.

Cone-bearing plants and flowering plants

Chapter Review

Chapter Summary

- The plant kingdom is divided into two big groups: vascular plants and nonvascular plants. Vascular plants have special cell tissue for transporting food and water. Nonvascular plants cannot move water and food between organs.

- Mosses and liverworts are simple, nonvascular plants. Mosses and liverworts like wet, usually shady, places.

- Ferns are simple, vascular plants. Ferns reproduce by spores. They also like wet, shady places.

- A seed contains a plant embryo and a food supply. It is covered by a protective coat. Seed plants are more complex than mosses, liverworts, and ferns. Seed plants are able to live in harsher environments than nonvascular plants. They have well-developed vascular tissue. They can send roots down to water. They do not use water for fertilization. And a seed can live a long time before either dying or growing.

- Seed plants are divided into two groups: cone-bearing plants and flowering plants.

Chapter Quiz

Write the answers to the following questions on a separate sheet of paper.

1. What are vascular plants?
2. Why do you think nonvascular plants are small and close to the ground?
3. Describe three characteristics of mosses.
4. What has become of the ferns from millions of years ago?
5. How does fertilization happen in ferns?
6. What is the difference between sexual and asexual reproduction?
7. Name five foods that you eat that come from seed plants.
8. Describe a seed.
9. Why does a seed have a better chance of surviving than a spore?
10. Into which two groups are seed plants divided?

Classifying Plants

On a separate sheet of paper, make a branching diagram showing the different plant classifications you learned about in this chapter. Include the following titles: "plant kingdom," "vascular plants," "nonvascular plants," "ferns," "seed plants," "flowering plants," and "cone-bearing plants."

Mad Scientist Challenge: Drawing Plants

Find a plant you like. You might find it growing outside, or you might find a picture of it in an encyclopedia. On a separate sheet of paper, draw a picture of the plant. Try to get all its parts in the picture. Write whether it is vascular or nonvascular. If it is vascular, say whether it is a fern or seed plant. If it is a seed plant, say whether it is cone-bearing or flowering.

Chapter 10

Plants at Work: Roots, Stems, and Leaves

Plants feed the entire earth. How do they create this food? How do they store the surplus nutrients?

Chapter Learning Objectives
- Name and define two kinds of roots.
- Name and define two kinds of stems.
- Explain the most important jobs of roots, stems, and leaves.
- Describe the big picture of photosynthesis.

Words to Know

blade   the broad flat part of a leaf

fibrous roots   many small, thin roots

herbaceous stems   green, soft stems

petiole   a thin rib that connects the leaf to the plant

phloem   a special tissue in roots and stems that carries food down the plant

root hairs   tiny hair-like structures on roots that absorb water into the plant

stomata   (singular, stoma) tiny pores on leaves that allow gases in and out of the leaves

taproot   one thick root

woody stems   hard brown stems, including tree trunks

xylem   a special tissue in roots and stems that carries water up the plant

Plants are like food factories. They make hundreds of trillions of pounds of sugar every year. When this simple sugar combines with other elements, it produces starches, proteins, and other necessary nutrients.

In this chapter, you will learn how plants carry out this food-making work. You will learn what parts roots, stems, and leaves play.

What Are Roots?

Have you ever heard stories of people getting lost in the wilderness? In many of these stories, the lost people survive on roots and berries. In fact, you eat roots all the time yourself. Potatoes, carrots, beets, turnips, and radishes are all roots.

Roots are one kind of plant organ. Roots are the parts of plants that grow underground. There is usually as much root underground as there is plant above ground. Plant roots usually grow as wide as the leaves or branches above ground.

There are two kinds of roots. A **taproot** is one thick root. Carrots and dandelions have taproots. **Fibrous roots** are many smaller roots. Grasses have fibrous roots.

Why do you think grasses are good for holding soil in place?

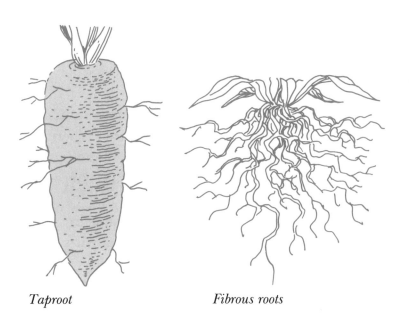

Taproot   *Fibrous roots*

Roots at Work

One important job of roots is to absorb water and minerals from the soil. Roots are covered with tiny structures called **root hairs**. If you study a carrot or a radish, you will see some small root hairs. However, by the time these roots get to the grocery store, most of the root hairs have been rubbed off.

Root hairs are the parts that do most of the absorbing of water. They have very thin cell walls. They absorb water very easily. The roots transport this water and minerals up to the stem of the plant.

Sometimes gardeners move plants. This is called *transplanting*. In doing this, they must be very careful not to damage the tiny root hairs.

Some plants use the roots to store food. Sometimes a plant makes more sugar than it needs. This sugar is changed into a starch. The starch is stored in the roots for later use. The carrots and turnips people eat are examples of this stored starch.

What do you think could happen to a plant if its root hairs are damaged?

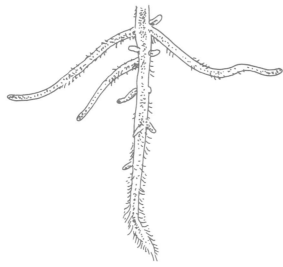

Root hairs

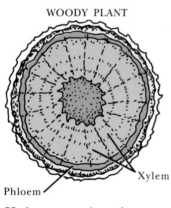

HERBACEOUS PLANT

Phloem
Xylem

WOODY PLANT

Phloem
Xylem

Herbaceous and woody stems

What Are Stems?

Rhubarb pie is made from the stems of rhubarb plants. Sugar is made from the stems of sugar cane plants. Celery, onions, bok choy, and asparagus are all stems that people eat.

Stems are the parts of plants that connect roots and leaves. There are two kinds of stems. **Herbaceous stems** are green and soft. They do not grow very big. Tomato, daffodil, and corn plants have herbaceous stems.

Woody stems are brown and hard. Tree trunks are woody stems. Many shrubs also have woody stems.

Amazing Biology

If you cut through a tree trunk, you will see many rings inside the trunk. These rings are bands of old plant cells. Each ring stands for one year of growth.

In the spring, there is a great deal of rainfall in most places. This causes trees to grow fast. The new cells grow big. In the summer, the weather becomes much drier. The new cells forming then are much smaller. The alternating groups of large and small cells form light and dark bands in tree trunks. A ring may be light on one side where it grew in the spring. The same ring may become dark where it grew in the winter. If you count these rings, you can figure out the age of a tree.

Stems at Work

The most important job of stems is to move or transport water, minerals, and food. Leaves need water delivered to them from the roots. Roots cannot carry out photosynthesis. So roots need food delivered to them from the leaves.

Xylem is a special kind of cell tissue that carries water and minerals. This tissue begins in the roots where the water and minerals are gathered. The xylem tissue delivers the water and minerals all the way up the plant. This tissue is made of long, thin tubes. It is at the center of stems.

Another special kind of tissue carries food down the stem to the roots. This special tissue is called **phloem**. The food travels in the form of sap.

Another job of stems is to hold plants upright. This keeps the leaves, which need the most light, closer to the sun. However, not all stems are upright. You may remember that fern stems are underground. Strawberry and cucumber stems lie along the ground.

Cutting a big chunk from the trunk of a tree will often kill the tree. Why do you think this happens?

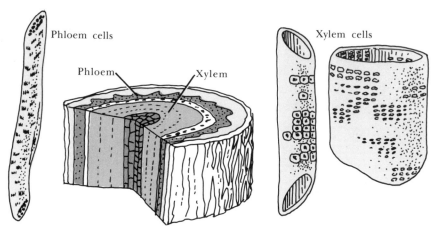

Xylem and phloem

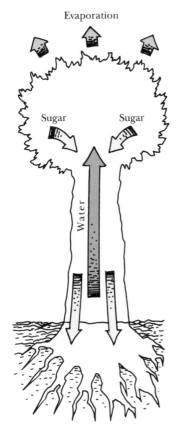

Evaporation

Sugar   Sugar

Water

Capillary action

On the Cutting Edge

Water travels from the soil upwards into tree trunks. Sometimes the water travels hundreds of feet. How does this water move against the force of gravity? Biologists do not know for sure. But they have some theories.

Part of the answer has to do with something called *capillary action.* Try putting a straw in a glass of water. The water will rise up the straw a little bit. The narrower the straw, the higher the water will rise. This is called capillary action. Xylem tissue is like a straw in the center of the tree trunk.

Still, capillary action doesn't explain how water travels hundreds of feet up a trunk. Another part of the answer has to do with evaporation. Lots of water evaporates off leaves. In the summer, a large tree can lose up to 250 quarts of water in one day! This makes the leaves dry out. The dry cells need to replace the water they've lost. So they pull more water up from the roots. The dryness of the leaves causes water to travel up the trunk.

Biology Practice

Write the answers to the following questions on a separate sheet of paper.

1. Name two roots you can eat.
2. Name one plant with a taproot.
3. Name one plant with fibrous roots.
4. What does xylem do?

Leaves at Work

Leaves are the green structures that grow off branches and stems. People eat many kinds of leaves, such as lettuce and cabbage. There are three main parts to leaves. The broad flat part is the **blade**. It is connected to the plant by a thin rib called a **petiole**. The even thinner ribs throughout the blade are called *veins*.

Leaves are the food makers for plants. Some stems can carry out photosynthesis. No roots can. Most of a plant's chlorophyll is in its leaves. So the leaf's most important job is to trap sunlight for photosynthesis.

Most leaves are broad and flat. This is so they can catch as much sunlight as possible. However, a few kinds of trees have needles instead of leaves.

Leaves of plants in hot, sunny climates tend to be small. They also tend to have thick skins. This protects them from water loss. In shady, wet places, leaves tend to grow big and thin. They need to gather all the sunlight they can. And they do not have to worry about drying out.

Types of leaves

Cactuses have needles instead of leaves. This is because they live in such hot, dry places. If they had leaves, they would lose too much water. Photosynthesis happens in the stems of the cactus. These stems have very thick skins. Very little moisture can escape.

Amazing Biology

Plants sweat just like animals do. Sweating is simply water evaporating off a body. The water vapor helps to cool the body. In fact, sweating is the main reason plants need water. They use a little water in photosynthesis. But most of the water a plant takes in is used to keep it cool. Why do you think plants need more water in the summertime?

How Leaves Breathe: Stomata

Water and food move up and down plant stems. But how do important gases, such as oxygen and carbon dioxide, move into and out of plants?

Plant leaves have many tiny *pores*. A pore is a little opening. These pores are called **stomata**. The carbon dioxide necessary for photosynthesis enters the stomata from the air. Wastes of photosynthesis—oxygen and water vapor—leave through the stomata.

Each stoma is guarded by two special cells. These cells are like doors to the stoma. They control the opening and closing of the stoma. When there is lots of water in the plant, these guard cells are swollen like balloons. This makes them pull back from the stoma. Water vapor can escape. Gases can come in.

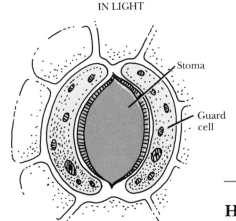

IN LIGHT

Stoma

Guard cell

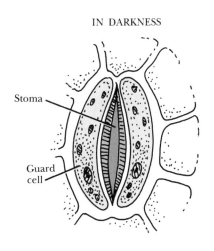

IN DARKNESS

Stoma

Guard cell

Opening and closing of stomata

But if the plant is dry, the guard cells flop together. This closes the openings of the stoma. The guard cells help keep a plant from drying out too much.

Photosynthesis: The Big Picture

Look again at the formula for photosynthesis:

sunlight + water + carbon dioxide = food + oxygen

You now know that the water comes from the plant roots. This is carried by xylem tissue up the plant stem to the leaves. The carbon dioxide enters the plant leaves through the stomata. Chlorophyll in the plant leaves absorbs sunlight.

The sunlight is used as energy to change the carbon dioxide and water into sugar (food). The waste oxygen leaves the plants through the stomata in the leaves. The food is used for plant growth and energy to carry out other plant jobs. Some food is delivered to the roots by phloem tissue. Extra food is stored in roots, stems, or leaves. This surplus food is what makes the fleshy part of many of the vegetables we eat, such as potatoes and carrots.

People in Biology: George Washington Carver

George Washington Carver, born a slave in 1864, became a great scientist. He was known around the world for his work with plants, especially peanuts. Carver was head of the Tuskegee Institute agricultural department in Alabama. He made more than 300 products from peanuts, including a milk substitute, printer's ink, and soap. He also developed more than 100 products from the sweet potato and 75 from the pecan.

Chapter Review

Chapter Summary

- Roots, stems, and leaves are all plant organs. Roots are the underground part of plants. Their main job is to absorb water. Most of the absorbing is done by tiny root hairs on roots. Roots also anchor plants to the ground. There are two kinds of roots. A taproot is one thick root. Fibrous roots are made of many thin roots.

- Most stems hold plants upright. This helps the leaves get more sunlight. The most important job of stems is to transport food, water, and minerals between the leaves and roots. Xylem tissue delivers water and minerals up the stem. Phloem tissue delivers food down the stem. There are two kinds of stems. Herbaceous stems are green and soft. Woody stems are hard and brown. Tree trunks are woody stems.

- Leaves make food for plants. They contain most of the plant's chlorophyll. Some of the food made in the leaf through photosynthesis is carried down the stem to the roots. The broad flat part of a leaf is the blade. The thin ribs throughout the leaf are the veins. The rib that attaches the leaf to the plant is called the petiole.

- Stomata are tiny pores on leaves. Oxygen, carbon dioxide, and water vapor can enter and leave plants through the stomata.

Chapter Quiz

Write the answers to the following questions on a separate sheet of paper.

1. Why can't roots carry out photosynthesis?
2. What plant organ is carrot cake made from?
3. What kind of tissue carries food down a plant?
4. What kind of tissue carries water and minerals up a plant?
5. Why do cactuses have needles instead of leaves?
6. How do oxygen, carbon dioxide, and water vapor enter and leave plants?
7. What is the job of guard cells?
8. Which plant organ contains most of the plant's chlorophyll?
9. Name one place where plants store extra food.
10. During a drought, do you think guard cells would be mostly open or mostly closed? Why?

Matching Plant Organs With Jobs

Number a separate sheet of paper from 1 to 3. Match each organ with its most important job. Write its letter next to the number.

1. _____ transporting food, water, and minerals   a. roots

2. _____ making food for the whole plant   b. stems

3. _____ absorbing water   c. leaves

Mad Scientist Challenge: Plant Organ Salad

On a separate sheet of paper, write a recipe for a plant organ salad. Include at least two kinds of roots, two kinds of stems, and two kinds of leaves.

Chapter 11

The Life Cycle of Seed Plants

Fruits and flowers don't make food. They don't perform photosynthesis. They don't transport water. What are they? Why do plants make them?

Chapter Learning Objectives
- Describe the purposes of flowers and fruits.
- Explain the life cycle of seed plants.
- List the parts of a flower.

Words to Know

nectar a sweet liquid in flowers that attracts insects

petals the parts of a flower that are often brightly colored

pistil the female part of a flower

plant ovary the flower part, at the bottom of the pistil, where egg cells are formed

pollen yellow grains that hold sperm

pollination the process by which pollen reaches the pistil in a flower

sepals the green leaf-like parts of a flower that support the petals

stamens the male parts of a flower

Have you ever sent or received flowers? Did you know you were sending or receiving the reproductive organs of plants? That is exactly what flowers are. Fruits, too, are part of a plant's reproductive cycle.

In this chapter, you will learn about plant reproduction. You will read how flowers, fruits, and cones help in the production of seeds.

The Parts of Flowers

Some flowers are much more showy than others. Roses, cherry blossoms, and irises are all examples of bright, beautiful flowers. Grasses, on the other hand, have flowers you cannot even see. The job of flowers, whether showy or not, is to help reproduce the plant.

The parts of flowers that are often brightly colored are called **petals**. The green leaf-like parts below the petals are called **sepals**.

In the center of the flower is a big structure that is often shaped like a vase. This is the female part of the flower. It is called the **pistil**. The fat part at the bottom of the pistil is the **plant ovary**. The ovary contains the egg cells.

Surrounding the pistil are the male parts of plants. These are thin stalks with round heads called **stamens**. The heads on the stamens are grains of **pollen**. Pollen hold the sperm cells.

A few kinds of plants have separate male and female flowers. In other words, some of the flowers only have female parts. Some of the flowers only have male parts.

A good way to learn is to look at the real thing. Find a flowering plant. Study the flower carefully. Find the petals, sepals, pistil, and stamens.

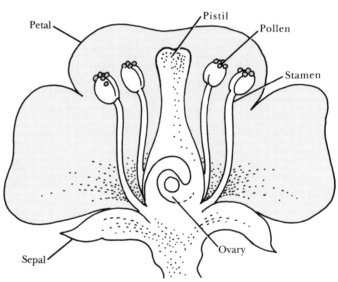

Parts of a flower

Pollination

For reproduction to take place, a sperm cell and egg cell must join. This means that a pollen grain must somehow get down in the ovary. The way this happens is called **pollination**.

Wind can play a big part in pollination. Pollen grains are light and dusty. Wind knocks them off the ends of stamens. Some of the flying pollen may land on the top of the pistil. The tops of pistils are sticky. This helps to catch pollen.

You can see that chance plays a big part in pollination. Most pollen grains carried by the wind do not land on any plant at all. A plant produces many, many grains of pollen. Only a very few will ever find their way to a pistil.

Animals also help in pollinating plants. Bees, butterflies, moths, birds, and bats are attracted to flowers. The bright color and the fragrance draw these animals. They come to drink the flower's **nectar**. This is a sweet liquid found in many flowers. As these animals brush the pollen, it sticks to their fur, feathers, or skin. Then the animals move on to other flowers. Pollen on their fur, feathers, or skin may fall off on another flower's pistil. In that way, a new flower is pollinated.

If pollen lands on the pistil of another type of plant, it is called *cross-pollination*. Plants can also *self-pollinate*. This happens when the pollen from a plant lands on a pistil of the same plant.

Pollen sticks to bees' legs as they collect nectar to make honey. While gathering the nectar, they pollinate many flowers.

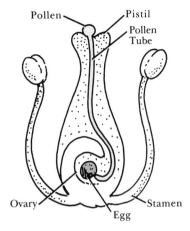

Pollen · Pistil
Pollen Tube
Ovary
Egg
Stamen

Fertilization

After a pollen grain lands on the sticky top of a pistil, the pollen begins to grow a long tube. This tube grows down into the ovary. The tube carries the sperm from the pollen. Once in the ovary, the tube releases the sperm. Then the egg is fertilized.

Soon an embryo begins to grow in the ovary. A covering grows around the embryo. Before long, a seed has formed. The seed contains the embryo and a food supply.

Fruits Protect Seeds

Most plants flower in the spring. This helps the new seeds to form. They will grow best if there is plenty of moisture and warmth. Once the embryo begins to grow, the flower falls off the plant. The ovary, which holds the seed, begins to get bigger. In time, the ovary grows into a fruit.

In biology, anything that covers a seed is called a *fruit*. A pea pod is a fruit (the pea is the seed). Plums, grapes, blackberries, cucumbers, tomatoes, beans, and lemons are all considered fruits by biologists. Fruits are simply plant ovaries containing the seeds.

Fruits have two important jobs. First, they protect the seed. Also, fruits help to scatter the seed.

Scattering Seeds

If all seeds fell right under the parent plant, they would have a hard time growing. They would be too crowded. They would die for lack of water, sunlight, and nutrients.

However, many seeds have special ways of getting some distance away from the parent plant. Fruits play a big part in this. Animals often gather fruits and carry them away to eat. Birds eat fruits, such as cherries, right off the tree. They may eat the seeds as well as the fruits. The seeds pass through their digestive systems. The birds may be far away before the seeds are dropped.

The wind also carries seeds away. Some fruits have wing-like structures to catch the air. They can glide like a paper airplane in the wind. Dandelion seeds fly away in the center of light, silky balls.

Other seeds have bristles or hooks. These bristles attach to people's clothing or to animal fur. You may have scattered some of these seeds yourself. After walking through a field, you may have found your socks or pants covered with small, brown, scratchy things. These are fruits and seeds. They have traveled on you away from the parent plant.

Coconuts are big fruits with seeds that float. They can float on the ocean away from the parent plant.

The Beginning of a New Plant

Plants produce many, many seeds. Only a very few grow into mature plants. The rest dry out and die.

If a seed lands in a good place, it will begin to grow. The embryo feeds on the food stored in the seed. When the time is right, the embryo will germinate. It begins to develop into a plant. Eventually, the embryo breaks out of the seed and grows roots in the soil. The new plant uses the roots to get nutrients in the soil. It uses the nutrients to grow.

Fruits are often brightly colored. The bright color attracts animals. The animals take the fruit and scatter the seeds.

Some seeds may remain in the soil a long time before the embryo begins to develop.

Reproduction in Cone-Bearing Plants

Cone-bearing plants do not have flowers. Instead, the cones themselves are the reproductive organs. These trees make female cones and male cones.

Female cones are usually bigger than male cones. Egg cells form in the female cones. Pollen, with sperm cells, forms in the male cones. Wind carries pollen to the female cones. The eggs are fertilized inside the cone.

Find a cone-bearing tree. Can you tell the difference between the male and female cones? Look for some pollen. It looks like yellow dust.

Biology Practice

Write the answers to the following questions on a separate sheet of paper.

1. What is the female part of a flower called?
2. Name two ways plants are pollinated.
3. List the two jobs of fruits.
4. List two ways seeds are scattered.

Asexual Reproduction in Seed Plants

All seed plants reproduce sexually. However, some can also reproduce asexually.

Some trees send up *suckers* from the roots. These are new shoots that grow straight out of the roots. They form new young trees.

Strawberry plants produce *runners*. These are stems that grow along the ground. Sometimes a runner grows roots. A new strawberry plant begins growing where the roots are. Mint plants have underground runners. In this way, mint plants reproduce very quickly.

Some plants grow from *bulbs*. Bulbs are plant stems with stored food. An onion is a bulb. Many flowers, such as daffodils and tulips, grow from bulbs.

Another way for plants to reproduce asexually is from *cuttings*. A cutting is a part of a plant stem or a leaf. It is cut off a plant and put in water. The cutting will grow roots and become a new plant.

Plants that are produced asexually are exactly like the parent plant. They have the same genetic makeup. For this reason, asexual reproduction is an important tool for farmers and gardeners. Suppose a gardener has a wonderful corn plant. The corn is bigger and sweeter than any she has ever grown. The gardener wishes all her corn plants were exactly like this one. If she takes a cutting of the corn plant, she will get an exact copy. That way she can control the quality of her corn crop.

On the Cutting Edge

Twelve and a half million tomato seeds circled our planet for nearly six years. They finally returned to Earth in 1990. What were these tomato seeds doing in space? They were one of many experiments being carried out aboard the Long Duration Exposure Facility. A shuttle crew brought the facility back to Earth.

Scientists wanted to find out how being in space might change tomato seeds. They decided to get students to help them. So after the seeds were retrieved from space, they were sent out to 64,000 teachers and 3,300,000 students. The students germinated the seeds.

What did the students find out? The space-exposed seeds germinated slightly faster — in 8 days as compared to 8.3 — than Earth-bound seeds. The seeds grew into delicious tomatoes.

Chapter Review

Chapter Summary

- Flowers are the reproductive parts of seed plants. The pistil, in the center of the flower, is the female part. It holds egg cells in the ovary at the bottom of the pistil. The stamens are the male parts. Pollen, at the top of stamens, hold sperm cells.

- The delivery of pollen to the pistil is called pollination. Wind, insects, and birds all help in pollination. The bright colors and fragrances of flowers attract animals. Animals come to flowers to drink the nectar.

- Once pollen has landed on a pistil, it begins to grow a long tube. This long tube grows down into the ovary. There it releases the sperm. The egg in the ovary becomes fertilized. As the seed grows, the flower falls away. The ovary grows large and fleshy. It becomes a fruit and protects the seed.

- Seeds are scattered by wind, water, or animals. If a seed lands somewhere favorable for growing, it will germinate. The plant will sprout leaves. It will grow roots.

- Reproduction in cone-bearing plants is much the same as in flowering plants. Instead of flowers, these plants produce male and female cones. The female cones produce egg cells. The male cones produce pollen containing sperm.

- Many seed plants can also reproduce asexually. This is done by way of suckers, runners, bulbs, or cuttings.

Chapter Quiz

Write answers to the following questions on a separate sheet of paper.

1. What are the female parts of plants called?
2. What role do stamens play in seed plant reproduction?
3. Name five animals that help with pollination.
4. Why do bees go to flowers in the first place?
5. What plant part grows into a fruit?
6. What are the two jobs of fruits?
7. Why is it important for seeds to be scattered?
8. Describe three different ways seeds can be scattered.
9. Why do most seeds dry out and die?
10. Name two types of asexual reproduction in seed plants.

Understanding the Parts of Flowers

Copy this picture of a flower on another piece of paper. Label the petals, sepals, pistil, ovary, and stamens.

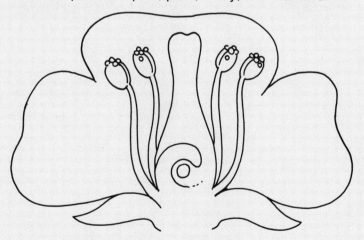

Mad Scientist Challenge: In Search of Fruits

Take a notebook and pen to a grocery store. Go to the produce part of the store. Find as many different kinds of fruit as you can. Make a list. Try to find some unusual ones.

Unit 3 Review

Answer the following questions on a separate sheet of paper.

1. What are the five characteristics of a plant?

2. What do plants need to live?

3. Why is photosynthesis important to all living things?

4. How do ferns reproduce?

5. What advantages do seed plants have?

6. What does a seed need to germinate?

7. What is the difference between taproots and fibrous roots?

8. Why are root hairs important?

9. What do xylem and phloem do?

10. What is pollination?

Animals: ~~sex~~
The Food Hunters

Unit 4

Chapter 12

Invertebrates: Animals Without Backbones

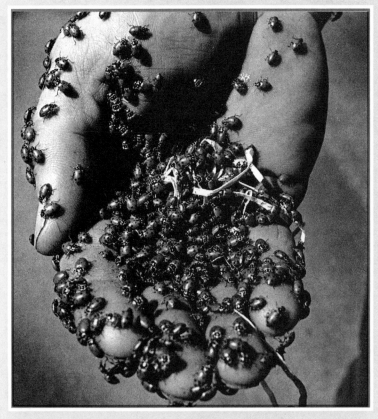

Insects, like these ladybugs, have a hard outer skin that is almost like armor. Why don't human beings have such a hard outer skin?

Chapter Learning Objectives
- Define vertebrates and invertebrates.
- Describe the main groups into which invertebrates are classified.
- Name three characteristics of invertebrate animals.

Words to Know

abdomen   the end part of an insect's body

appendages   parts that stick out from an organism, such as arms, legs, wings, claws, and feelers

arachnids   arthropods with four pairs of legs, such as spiders or scorpions

arthropods   animals with exoskeletons, segmented bodies, and jointed appendages, such as insects and arachnids

crustaceans   a group of arthropods, such as crabs and lobsters, that generally live in water

exoskeleton   a tough, stiff covering or shell around the body of an organism

host   an animal on or in which parasites live

invertebrates   animals without backbones

mollusks   animals with soft bodies that are not divided into segments, such as snails, oysters, and clams. Most *mollusks* have hard shells.

parasites   organisms that live on or inside other organisms

testes   the male organs that produce sperm cells

thorax   the middle part of an insect's body

vertebrates   animals with backbones

People are very complex animals. They have many, many parts. They have many kinds of specialized cells. They are able to do all kinds of things that other animals cannot do.

But sometimes people do not realize just how talented other animals are. For example, an ant has a larger brain in proportion to its body than any other animal. And an ant can lift 50 times its own body weight. That is the same as an average person lifting over 7,000 pounds!

In this chapter you will learn some facts about a special group of animals: those without backbones.

The Animal Kingdom

The animal kingdom has two main characteristics. First, all animals have many cells. These cells are specialized. In most animals, they are organized into tissues, organs, and systems. Neither protists, monera, nor fungi have specialized cells.

Second, animals all get their energy by eating other organisms. Animals cannot make their own food like plants. They must go out and hunt plants or animals to eat. So, animals must be able to move around. *You are not a plant because you cannot make your own food using energy from the sun.*

Animal Classification

The animal kingdom is broken into two main groups. The first group is made of simpler animals without backbones. Animals with no backbones are called **invertebrates**. Jellyfish, worms, starfish, snails, octopuses, insects, and spiders are all invertebrates. This chapter is about these animals.

In the next chapter you will read about animals *with* backbones. These animals are called **vertebrates**. Generally, vertebrate animals are more complex than invertebrate animals. Fishes, birds, bears, lizards, snakes, squirrels, and monkeys are all vertebrates.

What about humans? Are we invertebrates or vertebrates? If you have any question, feel down the center of your own back. What are the bumps that you are touching?

The Simplest Animals: Sponges

Sponges are animals that live in the ocean. They spend most of their lives anchored to a rock. There are many pores and openings in a sponge's body.

Sponges are the simplest kind of animal. They have a few kinds of specialized cells, such as covering cells. But they do not have any organs or systems.

Sea water washes right through a sponge's body. The sponge gets oxygen and tiny bits of food from this water. The water also washes away wastes.

Sponges are able to reproduce in a special asexual way. One sponge can be cut into ten pieces. Those ten pieces will grow into ten mature sponges. People who grow sponges to sell use this method. That way they can grow many sponges quickly.

Sponges also produce small offspring. The offspring swim away from the parent and find another rock. Then, they attach themselves to the new rock and grow into adult sponges.

Biologists used to think of sponges as plants. But sponges cannot carry out photosynthesis. They get their food out of the water. And, as offspring, they *do* swim freely in the sea.

Sponges are probably the simplest animals on Earth. Some biologists also believe they were the first animals on Earth.

Most sponges you buy in the store aren't natural sponges. They are made of plastic.

Sponges

A sea anemone

Jellyfish, Sea Anemones, and Coral

Jellyfish, sea anemones, and coral belong to another group of invertebrates. They are all alike in that their bodies are big sacks. This big sack has one opening, a mouth. Food goes in the mouth. Wastes also come out of the mouth.

Surrounding the mouth of a jellyfish are tentacles. These are like fleshy arms. Jellyfish tentacles have stingers on the ends. They use these stingers to catch small fish for food. First, the jellyfish catches the fish with its tentacles. Then it "stings" its catch. Poison in the stinger makes the animal unable to move. Then the jellyfish can eat its meal.

Jellyfish have no body systems. They have a few nerve cells. But they do not have a brain or an organized nervous system.

Corals are covered by a hard **exoskeleton**. They make this exoskeleton by using lime from the sea. This hard lime is often beautifully colored. People use it to make jewelry and other decorations.

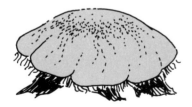

A jellyfish

On the Cutting Edge

In June 1991, the space shuttle *Columbia* went on a nine-day flight. Its purpose was to study how people and animals adapt to space. Joining the four men and three women aboard the *Columbia* were 2,400 jellyfish. Why the jellyfish? The scientists studied how jellyfish respond to being in an environment with very little gravity. Although some of the jellyfish swam in circles and others were not as active, most of the jellyfish were able to reproduce and develop normally in space.

Three Kinds of Worms

All worms are invertebrates. There are three groups of worms: flatworms, roundworms, and segmented worms.

• Flatworms

Most flatworms are **parasites**. A parasite is an animal that lives on or in another animal, called its **host**. The parasite feeds off the flesh and blood of the host.

Tapeworms are a common type of flatworm. A tapeworm is a long flatworm with a small head. Hooks and suckers on its head are used to attach itself to its host. Tapeworms can grow as long as 20 yards!

Not all flatworms are parasites, though many are. The *planarian* is a flatworm that is not a parasite. It lives in streams and ponds.

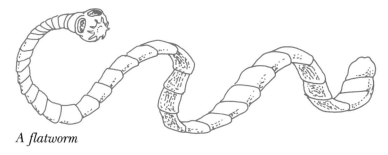

A flatworm

Biology Alert

People can get tapeworms from eating infected beef. Cows get them from eating grass that has tapeworm eggs in it.

But most people in this country no longer have to worry about getting tapeworms. Meat-packing plants are regularly inspected. Beef growers take measures to keep their cows free from infection.

• Roundworms

Roundworms are more complex than flatworms. They have a simple digestive system. This means they have a mouth where food enters. And they have an anus where wastes leave. A tube connects the mouth and anus. As food moves through the body, some passes through the walls of the tube. This food goes to the other cells in the worm's body. The roundworm's nervous system is well-developed.

Biology Alert

Trichina is a parasitic roundworm. It can make people very sick. People get this parasite from eating pork that is not well-cooked. The parasite causes serious muscle pains, fever, and weakness. Sometimes it even causes death. Farmers can help stop the spread of this parasite. They can do this by cooking garbage before feeding it to pigs.

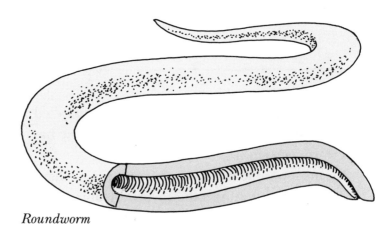

Roundworm

• Segmented Worms

The common earthworm—the one used for fishing—is a segmented worm. Its body is divided into 100 to 180 ring-like segments. Earthworms move by means of tiny bristles. They use these bristles to push and pull their way along. These animals are much more developed than flatworms or roundworms. Earthworms have a head, tail, mouth, intestines, blood, nerves, and even a tiny brain.

Earthworms live underground. When it is cold outside, they can dig as far as two yards below the surface. By doing this they avoid hard frosts.

As earthworms burrow through soil, some of that soil passes right through their bodies. This is the way earthworms feed. Organic matter in the soil is used as food. Rock particles in the soil help with digestion. They grind up the food. What isn't used by the worm's body passes out the anus.

The circulatory system in animals carries blood throughout the body. Blood delivers food and oxygen to all the body cells. Most animals have a heart that pumps the blood. Earthworms have five hearts!

Earthworms are neither male nor female. They have both male and female sex organs. This means they have **testes**, the male organ that makes sperm. And they also have ovaries, the female organ that makes egg cells. When they mate, the two worms give each other sperm.

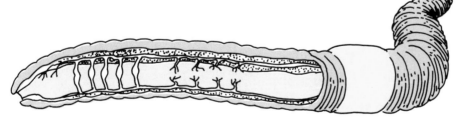

Earthworm

Most starfish live from three to five years.

Spiny-Skinned Animals

Starfish, sea urchins, and sand dollars all belong to another group of animals. They live in the ocean. They all have a tough skin. This skin is covered with spines.

Starfish have tube feet. They use these to hold onto rocks. They also use them to grasp and pull open clams and oysters. Once a starfish has opened a shellfish, it does a most unusual thing. It opens its mouth and pushes its stomach out of its mouth! The stomach goes into the clam or oyster shell. There it digests the food. Then the starfish swallows its own stomach again.

Starfish have a digestive system, a circulatory system, and a nervous system.

Biology Practice

Five animals are listed below. On a separate sheet of paper, write a sentence or two saying how each one gets its food.

1. sponge
2. jellyfish
3. tapeworm
4. earthworm
5. starfish

Mollusks

Have you ever eaten raw oysters? Some people consider them a delicacy. Oysters belong to a group of animals called **mollusks**. Most mollusks can be tasty food for people. Clams, oysters, squid, octopus, and snails are all mollusks.

All mollusks have soft bodies. Most of them have shell coverings, though squids and octopuses do not. The shells form on a special part of the skin called the *mantle*. Most mollusks live in salt water. Some snails, however, live in fresh water or on land. Mollusks come in all sizes. Giant squids, as heavy as two tons, have been found.

Besides being eaten as food, many mollusks are helpful to people. Oyster shells are crushed and fed to chickens. The shells are a source of calcium.

Oysters also make pearls. A pearl starts as a bit of sand or a tiny worm. This gets inside the oyster. Special shell-forming cells coat the bit of sand or worm. These cells keep dividing, making more and more shell material. The pearl grows bigger and bigger.

Snails can be real pests to gardeners. If there are a lot of them, they can eat most of a garden in one night. However, they are a big help in aquariums. Snails eat the algae off the glass sides. This keeps the aquarium clean for clear viewing.

Mollusks are the largest group of water animals.

Arthropods

Insects, spiders, crabs, lobsters, scorpions, centipedes, and millipedes are all **arthropods**. These animals all have three things in common. First, they are covered with a shell, or exoskeleton. Second, they have bodies that are divided into segments. Third, they have jointed **appendages**. Appendages are body parts that stick out such as arms, legs, wings, claws, and feelers. Jointed appendages are ones that can bend at certain places.

Insects are the biggest group of arthropods. In fact, they are the biggest group of animals living on land. There are about 700,000 different kinds of insects. Grasshoppers, flies, lice, butterflies, beetles, and bees are just a few. Scientists guess that there are about 1,000,000,000,000,000,000 insects living on Earth at any given moment.

The bodies of insects are divided into three parts: a head, a **thorax**, or a chest area, and an **abdomen**, the end part. The picture on this page shows these three parts on a grasshopper. Insects also have three pairs of legs. Usually they have wings, too.

Mites are tiny arthropods. They live in the roots of people's hairs. They feed on bacteria there. You may have some on you right now.

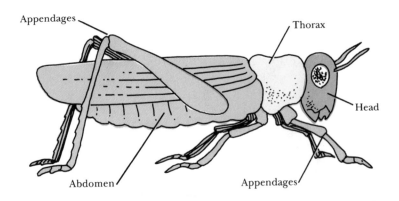

Appendages

Thorax

Head

Abdomen

Appendages

Most insects are helpful. For one thing, they pollinate flowering plants. But mosquitoes can carry malaria, and others carry sleeping sickness. Flies and cockroaches bring germs from garbage and animal wastes into homes. Insects can also destroy farm crops.

Spiders are another kind of arthropod. They help keep insect numbers down. Spiders eat insects. People often mistake spiders for insects, but they are really **arachnids**. Spiders have only two body sections. And they have four, rather than three, pairs of legs.

Lobsters and crabs are in another class of arthropods called **crustaceans**. Crustaceans are a very popular seafood.

A flea can jump 60 times its own body length. If you could jump 60 times your own body length, how far could you jump?

Chapter Review

Chapter Summary

- The two main characteristics of animals are 1) they are made of many, specialized cells; and 2) they must eat other organisms for energy.

- Animals are broken into two main groups, invertebrates and vertebrates.

- Sponges are the simplest animals alive. They are invertebrates that live in the sea. They get their food and oxygen from water as it washes through them.

- Jellyfish, corals, and sea anemones are invertebrates with sack-like bodies and tentacles. Jellyfish catch small fish with their tentacles.

- There are three main kinds of worms: flatworms, roundworms, and segmented worms. Most flatworms are parasites. These are animals that live off other animals called hosts.

- Starfish, sea urchins, and sand dollars all belong to another group of invertebrates. They live in the ocean. They all have a tough, spiny skin.

- Oysters, clams, snails, octopuses, and squid are all mollusks. These invertebrates have soft bodies. Most of them have shell coverings and live in salt water. Many people like to eat mollusks.

- Insects, spiders, crabs, lobsters, scorpions, centipedes, and millipedes are all arthropods. These animals all have three things in common: exoskeletons, segmented bodies, and jointed appendages.

- Insects are the biggest group of arthropods. The bodies of insects are divided into three parts. They also have three pairs of legs. Usually they have wings.

Chapter Quiz

Write the answers to the following questions on a separate sheet of paper.

1. Why can't animals use energy from sunlight to make their own food?
2. What is the difference between invertebrates and vertebrates?
3. Give two reasons why sponges are not plants.
4. What are parasites?
5. Describe the digestive system of a roundworm.
6. How do earthworms move?
7. Name three ways that mollusks are useful to people.
8. What is an exoskeleton? Which kind of animals have exoskeletons?
9. List all the appendages of a grasshopper.
10. What is the difference between an insect and a spider?

Animal Words

On a separate sheet of paper, write a sentence using each of the following words. Your sentence should show that you understand what the word means.

1. invertebrate
2. parasite
3. appendage
4. thorax

Mad Scientist Challenge: Science Research

Choose one of the invertebrate animals discussed in this chapter. Look up the animal in an encyclopedia. You may want to find library books as well. Write a short report on the animal's characteristics. Cover the following points:

1) What does the animal look like?
2) How does the animal move?
3) What does the animal eat?

Chapter 13

The Cold-Blooded Vertebrates

Crocodiles and alligators don't look much like snakes or fish. Yet biologists put all these animals in the same group. Why?

Chapter Learning Goals

- Describe the jobs of two body systems.
- Explain the difference between warm-blooded and cold-blooded animals.
- Describe two important features of fish, amphibians, and reptiles.

Words to Know

amphibians   cold-blooded vertebrates that live part of their lives in water and part on land

dinosaurs   a group of reptiles that died off millions of years ago

gills   organs used by fish for getting oxygen from water

skeleton   a group of bones that work together to support an organism's body

What makes you different from a jellyfish? A spider? A sponge? All those animals you just studied are in one big group of animals called invertebrates, or animals without backbones. You, along with crocodiles, birds, fish, snakes, and whales, are in the other big group called *vertebrates*. You and all other vertebrates have backbones.

The Body Systems of Vertebrates

A backbone is part of the **skeleton**. A skeleton is a structure made of bone. These bones work together to support an organism's body. The bones also protect many organs. The brain, for example, is surrounded by a big bone called the skull. The heart is protected by the rib cage.

The skeletal system is just one kind of system in vertebrate animals. In this and the next few chapters you also will learn about the muscular, digestive, respiratory, circulatory, and reproductive systems of animals. The chart below tells you the function of each of these systems in the bodies of vertebrate animals.

System	Function of System
skeletal	supports the body and protects organs
muscular	moves the body
digestive	breaks food down into nutrients for the body
respiratory	gets oxygen into the body
circulatory	moves food and oxygen throughout the body in blood
reproductive	makes offspring

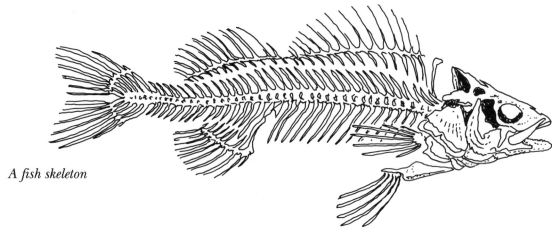

A fish skeleton

Cold-Blooded and Warm-Blooded

This chapter is about the *cold-blooded* vertebrates. Cold-blooded animals do not have a constant body temperature. Their bodies take on the temperature of their environment. Fish, for example, are cold-blooded. If they are swimming in cold water, their bodies are cold. If they are swimming in warm water, their bodies are warm.

You are *warm-blooded.* That means you maintain a constant body temperature. The normal temperature for humans is about 98.6 degrees. Fat, feathers, and fur all help warm-blooded animals to maintain their body temperatures. Generally, warm-blooded animals must eat more than cold-blooded ones. That is because warm-blooded animals use a lot of energy trying to stay warm. Warm-blooded animals must maintain their body temperature.

This table shows five kinds of vertebrates you will study.

Do you think a mouse is cold-blooded or warm-blooded? How about a cricket?

Class	Body Coverings	Appendages	Blood
Fish	Scales	Fins	cold
Amphibians	Moist, slimy skin	Legs	cold
Reptiles	Scales	Legs	cold
Birds	Feathers	Legs, wings	warm
Mammals	Hair or fur	Legs	warm

Amazing Biology

Cold-blooded animals must use the environment to change temperature. On a cold day, snakes will lie in the sun. This is because they are trying to raise their body temperature. On a hot day, they will lie in the shade to lower their body temperature.

Fish

Shark, salmon, goldfish, bass, trout, cod, red snapper, and catfish are all fish. These cold-blooded vertebrates all live in water. Most of them have slim, pointed bodies. This shape helps them cut through the water better. They use their fins for swimming.

Fish also have scales covering their bodies. These scales have rings on them. Each ring stands for one year of growth. You can count the number of rings on a fish scale. This will tell you how old a fish is. It is a lot like counting the rings of growth in a tree trunk.

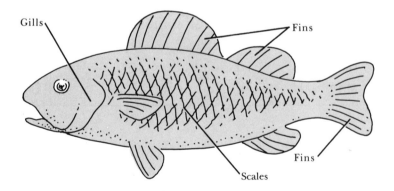

Another special feature of fish is **gills**. Gills are a major organ of their respiratory system. Fish do not have lungs. Because they live under water, fish cannot breathe oxygen from the air. Instead, they must get oxygen out of the water. Getting oxygen from the water is the function of gills.

To get oxygen, a fish pumps water over its gills. There is oxygen dissolved in the water. The oxygen passes through very thin parts of the gills into the blood cells. Then the blood cells carry the oxygen to the other cells in the fish's body. Carbon dioxide, a waste product, passes from the blood cells out through the gills.

Female fish reproduce by laying eggs. Some lay millions of eggs. The male fish swims over the eggs. It releases a substance that has sperm in it. Some of this sperm fertilizes some of the eggs. Fish eggs have no shells to protect them. They can be eaten by other fish. Many of them never get fertilized.

Most fish eat plants and smaller fish. Some of them eat a type of algae called *plankton.* Some fish eat the insects that land on the water.

Blue-green algae and underwater plants produce oxygen by photosynthesis. Even the underwater environment depends on photosynthesis for food and oxygen.

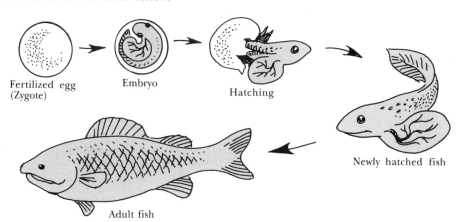

Fertilized egg
(Zygote)

Embryo

Hatching

Newly hatched fish

Adult fish

The life cycle of a fish

Amphibians

Frogs, toads, and salamanders are all **amphibians**. Amphibians can live both on land and in water. Amphibians live the early parts of their lives in water and the latter parts of their lives on land. These vertebrates have slimy skin and no scales. They are cold-blooded.

Does a frog need to use a lot of energy to stay warm?

The frog is a good amphibian to study. Frogs live near fresh water. They eat live insects and worms. The frog's tongue is especially useful in catching insects. The tongue is attached to the front of the mouth. (Most animals, like you, have a tongue attached to the back of the mouth.) Also, the frog's tongue is very sticky. This makes it easier to reach out and snatch an insect.

Frogs usually reproduce in the spring. The female lays eggs in water. Since the eggs have no shells, they would dry out if they were laid on land. The male frog fertilizes the eggs by dropping sperm over them.

The fertilized eggs develop into little organisms called *tadpoles*. Tadpoles have a tail and live in the water. They have gills for getting oxygen from the water. However, as the tadpole develops, it loses its gills. In their place, frogs develop lungs for breathing air! The tadpole also loses its tail and grows legs.

Once it has lungs instead of gills, the frog must live mostly on land. It can swim in water. But to breathe, a frog must come to the surface. On land, it breathes just as a human being does. Air is breathed into the lungs. The oxygen passes into the tiny blood vessels that surround the lungs. The blood cells absorb the oxygen. The circulatory system carries the oxygen to all parts of the body. Waste carbon dioxide is carried in the blood to the lungs. The carbon dioxide is breathed out into the air.

The muscular system is also involved in breathing. Chest muscles lift the ribs and expand the lungs so they can suck in the air.

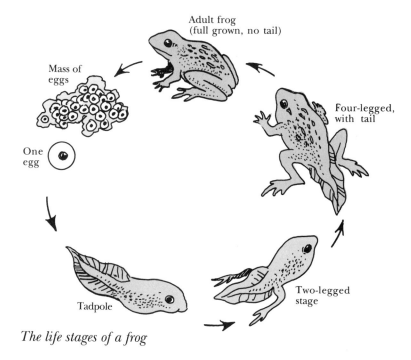

The life stages of a frog

Biology Practice

Answer the following questions about fish and amphibians on a separate sheet of paper.

1. What is similar about the way that fish and amphibians get oxygen?
2. What is different about the way that fish and amphibians get oxygen?
3. What is similar about the way fish and amphibians fertilize egg cells?
4. What is different about the way that young fish and amphibians develop?

All dinosaurs weren't big. The compsognathus was less than 3 feet long.

On the Cutting Edge

Millions of years ago, there were reptiles called **dinosaurs**. Among them were the biggest animals to ever live on land. One kind, the brontosaurus, was 80 feet long. It weighed over 100,000 pounds.

What happened to these great animals? Some biologists think that a huge meteorite fell to Earth. A *meteorite* is a rock from outer space. When this meteorite fell, say scientists, it caused great clouds of dust. The clouds blocked the sun for months. This caused many plants to die. With no plants to eat, many animals—including the dinosaurs—also died.

Tyrannosaurus rex

Tyrannosaurus rex was about 40 feet long.

Reptiles

The dinosaurs are long gone. But other reptiles still live on Earth. Lizards, snakes, turtles, crocodiles, and alligators are all reptiles. These are cold-blooded, vertebrate animals. They breathe air with their lungs and live mostly on land.

The skin of reptiles is made of dry scales. These scales help reptiles keep the water in their bodies. If an animal loses too much of the water in its body, it will die. The scales also protect the animals from rough surfaces such as sand and rocks.

Except for snakes, reptiles have four legs. Most reptiles have clawed toes.

Snakes have long round bodies and no legs. The skeleton of a snake includes a skull, backbone, and ribs. Pythons have as many as 400 bones in their bodies.

Snakes have teeth, but they do not tear or chew their food. They swallow other animals whole. The jaws of snakes can open very wide. Pythons have eaten whole kangaroos and pigs!

Black rat snakes may be 6 feet long.

Snakes' teeth are slanted backwards. They are used to hold animals in their mouths. Some snakes have *fangs*. These are hollow teeth. Poison flows through the fangs. The poison will paralyze an animal. Then the snake can swallow it. The venom of the king cobra is very poisonous. Just a third of an ounce can kill 150 people.

In reproduction, reptiles fertilize eggs inside the female. However, development of the young happens outside the female's body. Reptiles lay leathery eggs on land. The soft shells protect the eggs. They keep the eggs from drying out.

A snake has very powerful muscles to swallow the food it eats.

Amazing Biology

Crocodiles keep five pounds of rocks in their stomachs. These rocks are part of the crocodile's digestive system. The rocks break up the crocodile's food.

Snake eggs hatching

Chapter Review

Chapter Summary

- Vertebrates are animals with backbones. Vertebrates have several body systems: skeletal, muscular, digestive, respiratory, circulatory, and reproductive.

- A cold-blooded vertebrate's body temperature changes with its environment. The three main classes of cold-blooded vertebrates are fish, amphibians, and reptiles.

- Fish live in water and have bodies suited for swimming. They have fins as appendages. They have scales covering their bodies. Fish use gills for getting oxygen out of the water. Fertilization and development of the young both happen outside the female's body.

- Amphibians spend the early parts of their lives in water. When they are young, they have gills and fish-like bodies. When they grow legs and develop lungs, they move on to land to live their adult lives. Amphibians eat insects and worms. Reproduction and development of the young both happen outside the female's body.

- Reptiles live on land. They breathe air and have lungs. Their skin is made of dry scales, and most have clawed toes. Snakes have no appendages at all. The female's eggs are fertilized inside her body. She then lays leathery eggs.

Chapter Quiz

Write the answers to the following questions on a separate sheet of paper.

1. Are you cold-blooded or warm-blooded? Explain what that means.
2. What are some ways that warm-blooded animals stay warm?
3. How do fish get oxygen into their bodies?
4. Why do fish lay so many eggs?
5. How can you tell the age of a fish?
6. What parts of a young frog's body change as it grows older?
7. Why is a salamander an amphibian and not a reptile?
8. How do lizards get oxygen into their bodies?

Cold-Blooded Vertebrates

Cold-blooded animals must use the environment to change their body temperatures. For each animal listed below, describe one way it could get warm and one way it could cool off.

frog   lizard   shark

Mad Scientist Challenge: Fish

Go to a pet store or aquarium and look at the fish. Pick a fish you like. On a separate sheet of paper, write a short paragraph about the fish. Does it live in salt water or fresh water? What does it eat? What animals eat it? Do people catch it and eat it?

Chapter 14

The Warm-Blooded Vertebrates

Bald eagles have powerful wings and large hooked beaks.

Chapter Learning Objectives

- Name the five characteristics of mammals.
- List four important features of birds.
- Describe the main groups of mammals.

You are a warm-blooded vertebrate. Warm-blooded vertebrates use a great deal of energy maintaining a constant body temperature. When it is hot, you sweat to cool your body temperature. When it is cold, you shiver to raise your body temperature.

In this chapter you will read about two classes of warm-blooded vertebrates: birds and mammals.

Birds

Birds are warm-blooded vertebrates. Their body temperatures remain constant. They have lungs for breathing air. They also have four appendages—two wings and two legs. Their bodies are covered with feathers. The feathers help keep the bird warm.

Birds have several characteristics that make them able to fly. First, they have wings. The breast muscles of most birds are very strong. This helps them beat their wings. And birds have hollow bones. This keeps their bodies very light. They also have many air sacs inside their bodies. These air sacs help keep them light, too.

Have you ever looked at a ham bone? Was it hollow?

Amazing Biology

People sometimes say, "You eat like a bird!" They mean that you don't eat much. But they are wrong to use birds as examples of small eaters. Birds work very hard at flying. They burn up a lot of energy. Most birds eat their own weight in food every day! How many pounds of food would you have to eat each day to "eat like a bird"?

Fertilization takes place inside the female bird. The female then lays hard-shelled, fertilized eggs. Either the male or female bird sits on the eggs to keep them warm until they hatch. This takes several weeks. Once born, young birds need great care or they will die. The parents feed and guard them.

Since birds are warm-blooded, their eggs must be kept warm. For example, the emperor penguin lays only one egg at a time. It must be kept warm in the cold climate of the Antarctic. Both penguin parents take turns keeping the egg warm. They hold it on their feet. Their stomachs hang down over the egg to keep it warm.

Birds building a nest

Many birds build nests to protect their eggs. Birds build nests from mud, grass, and twigs. Try to find a nest in a neighborhood tree.

Migration

Some birds, such as the bobwhite, live in the same place all year. Others, such as the robin, fly to warmer areas in the winter. This regular travel pattern is called **migration**. Most migratory birds go north to feed and nest in the spring and summer. They return south for the winter.

Birds that migrate use the same routes every year. Biologists think that they use the stars as guides. The arctic tern flies south in the fall to the Antarctic. In the spring, it flies all the way back to the Arctic. The bird makes a round trip of over 20,000 miles every year.

To navigate *is to steer or direct along a course.*

On the Cutting Edge

In 1953, some scientists caught a manx shearwater near England. They took the bird to Boston, Massachusetts. There they let the bird go. After 12-1/2 days, the bird returned to its nest near England. It had flown back across the Atlantic Ocean, on a route it had never traveled before. And it found its own nest—a single nest in a single tree—across a distance of 3,000 miles!

How did the bird know how to get home? Scientists are still not sure. Migrating birds may use the sun and stars to navigate. Scientists believe that certain birds are guided by the Earth's magnetic pull. Some birds circle to get their bearings. They are *orienting* themselves. Orienting means they are determining where they are and which way is home. Some birds may use landmarks to find the way. But this does not explain how a bird can fly home over a route it has never taken before.

Some people use this navigational ability of birds. They train homing pigeons to deliver messages. But we still don't know exactly how the birds navigate.

Beaks and Feet

Birds do not have teeth. They have beaks or bills instead. Bird beaks come in many shapes. Ducks have broad flat bills. These bills help ducks to strain water for food. Hawks have sharp, hooked beaks. These are used for catching and tearing meat. Other birds have strong beaks for cracking open seeds. Still others have long needle-like beaks for digging insects out of trees. The heron has a long pointed beak for fishing.

Birds have different kinds of feet, too. Swimming birds have webs on their feet. Birds that walk in water a lot, like herons, have long legs. They also have webbed feet to walk on mud. Meat eaters, like owls and hawks, have long sharp claws. Robins have toes pointing in different directions. These help the robins to grip tree branches while they sit.

Notice how well certain body parts are designed to match the animal's environment.

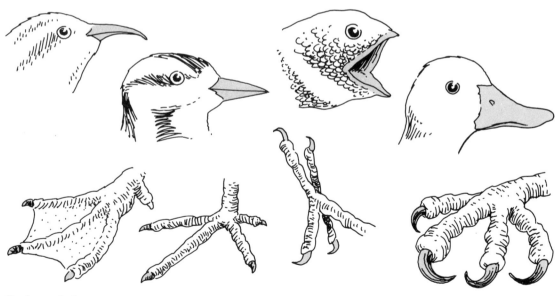

Beaks and claws

Biology Practice

On the left is a list of body systems. On the right is a list of details about birds. Number a separate sheet of paper from 1 to 5. Match each detail with the body system it is describing. Write a letter next to each number.

1. ___ skeletal   a. A bird eats its own weight in food every day.

2. ___ respiratory   b. Eggs are fertilized inside the female bird's body.

3. ___ reproductive   c. A bird's breast is very muscular.

4. ___ muscular   d. A bird's bones are hollow.

5. ___ digestive   e. Birds have lungs for getting oxygen.

What Are Mammals?

Mammals are highly developed, hairy, warm-blooded animals that feed on their mother's milk when young. Humans, bears, giraffes, mice, bats, deer, cats, dogs, whales, and raccoons are all mammals.

Mammals have two sets of appendages. Mammals that live in the sea have flippers. Mammals that walk have legs. People have arms. Many mammals have tails. All mammals breathe air through lungs.

They also have well-developed lips and teeth. Some mammals have special teeth for ripping and tearing. Others have special teeth for cutting and gnawing. Flat teeth, like the ones you have in back of your mouth, are for grinding.

The Five Characteristics of Mammals

Mammals all share five important characteristics.

1. *Mammals have hair on their bodies.* Dogs, tigers, antelopes, and many other mammals are covered with fur. Humans only have a little hair on their bodies. A few mammals, such as whales and dolphins, also have very little hair. However, these sea mammals are born covered with a fuzz. And as adults they still have whiskers.

2. *Mammals give birth to live young.* This means that they do not lay eggs. At birth, their babies are fully developed infant mammals.

3. *Mammals feed their young with milk from the mother's breasts.* All female mammals have *mammary glands.* This is where the word *mammal* comes from. These glands produce milk. All mammals feed their young with this milk.

4. *Mammals care for their young until they can care for themselves.* Most newly born animals are on their own from the start. Mammals, however, feed and protect their young. Many teach their young how to hunt, clean, and protect themselves.

5. *Mammals have big brains.* They are the most intelligent group of animals on Earth.

How do you know a chicken isn't a mammal?

Biology Alert

Dolphins are one of the most intelligent mammals on Earth. Nearly 100,000 dolphins were killed every year when they accidentally got caught in tuna nets. In April 1990, the three largest tuna sellers in the United States announced that they would stop using tuna fishing methods that hurt dolphins.

Unusual Mammals

There are about 5,000 kinds of mammals on Earth. Most live on land. Bats are unusual mammals because they can fly. Whales, porpoises, seals, and dolphins are unusual because they live in the sea.

The smallest bats weigh only about 1/20 of an ounce.

Amazing Biology

Bats are scary to many people. Their wings are made from their long finger bones. Skin stretches across these bones to make wings. Bats live in groups. They usually sleep, hanging upside down in caves, during the day. They become active at night.

One kind of bat is very dangerous to other mammals. Vampire bats live off blood. They wait until a large animal is sleeping. Then they bite the animal and lap up the blood that flows. The vampire bat's saliva has a special substance in it. This substance keeps blood from clotting. The animal wound does not heal up. This way, the bat gets more blood.

Most bats do little harm to people or crops.

Shrews are the smallest mammals. Whales are the largest. The blue whale is the largest animal that has ever lived. It can weigh more than 200,000 pounds.

Some mammals seem a lot like fish. Why aren't they grouped that way? For one thing, they breathe through lungs. They do not have gills. Whales must come to the surface to get oxygen. And whales give birth to live young. The infant whale is fed milk from the mother. Whales are warm-blooded. Thick layers of fat on their bodies help them stay warm in the cold seas.

The duck-billed platypus and the spiny anteater are also unusual mammals. They hatch eggs. But they are still mammals because the young are fed milk from the mother's mammary glands.

The pouched mammals are also unusual mammals. Kangaroos and opossums are a part of this group. They give birth to underdeveloped young. After being born, these little ones crawl up the mother's belly. They climb into a pouch there. In this pouch they nurse on the mother's milk. Finally, when they are fully developed, they crawl out of the pouch.

A baby kangaroo is called a joey.

Other Kinds of Mammals

The largest group of mammals is the rodents. These include rats, mice, squirrels, and beavers. They have sharp teeth for gnawing and cutting. They also reproduce very quickly.

Hoofed mammals are another group. These include horses, pigs, sheep, camels, cows, and deer. The hooves are really just overgrown toenails. These animals usually live in groups. Most of them eat vegetables. Many "chew their cud." This means that they can bring food up out of their stomach after they swallow it. Then they can chew it again for a long time.

Amazing Biology

Many hoofed mammals often have horns or antlers. These are used for protection. Antlers fall off each year. The animals grow a new set every spring. The bull moose cleans and polishes its antlers by rubbing them on trees. Then it uses them to fight other bulls to win females.

The Asiatic elephant has the longest pregnancy of any mammal. It carries a baby for about two years before the calf is born.

Elephants are the largest land animals. Today there are only two kinds of elephants on Earth: the African elephant and the Asiatic elephant. However, there used to be more than thirty kinds.

On the Cutting Edge

Isabel the elephant lives in a rain forest in Cameroon, on the west coast of Africa. Yet a scientist at the Bronx Zoo, 5,000 miles away, keeps track of her every step. In June of 1992, Isabel became the first rain forest animal to wear a satellite-tracked radio collar. The scientist uses a computer to follow Isabel and learn more about how elephants live.

Meat-eating mammals include wolves, seals, raccoons, dogs, lions, and bears. These mammals have claws and sharp teeth for tearing meat. They are good hunters because they can move fast and have good eyesight.

Is a cat a meat-eating mammal?

Amazing Biology

You might think that humans are the only animals that use deodorant. If so, it may surprise you to learn that cats use deodorant every day. Cats spend hours cleaning themselves by licking their fur coats. Their saliva has a special substance in it. This substance is a kind of deodorant. This is the reason dogs often have an odor, but cats usually do not.

The Primates

You are a member of the most highly developed group of mammals. In fact, you are the most intelligent kind of organism on Earth. You are a **primate**. Monkeys, chimpanzees, and gorillas are also in this group.

Primates have several characteristics that set them apart from other mammals. They have hands with movable fingers. They also have thumbs that can touch all the other fingers on the same hand. This is important because it makes it possible to pick up things easily.

The thumb is very important. It allows primates to grasp and hold things. Because the thumb bends the opposite way of the other fingers, it is called the opposing digit.

Many animals, such as horses, fish, and many types of birds, have eyes on the sides of their face. Each eye sees something a little different. These animals see only a flat world. But primates and some other mammals have both eyes on the front of their face. Both eyes are looking forward. The two eyes combine to create a single image in the brain. The combined image has *depth*, also known as the third dimension.

More than 200 species of mammals are classified as primates. The smallest primate, the tarsier, is only 3 to 5 inches long. The human being is the tallest primate.

Most non-human primates live in warm parts of the world. Some of these animals, like baboons, spend a lot of time on the ground. But most non-human primates live in trees.

Nearly all primates, including humans, live in social groups.

Humans

Humans are the most highly developed primates. We walk upright all the time. We have the best control over our fingers and thumbs. And we have the biggest brains.

The next six chapters are about a very important primate: you. You will learn about the body systems of humans.

Primates

Chapter Review

Chapter Summary

- Birds and mammals are two classes of warm-blooded animals. Their body temperature remains constant.

- Birds are able to fly because of wings, strong breast muscles, hollow bones, and air sacs inside their bodies. Flying takes a lot of energy, so birds must eat a lot. Fertilization takes place inside the female bird. She lays hard-shelled eggs. The parents protect and feed young birds.

- Birds' beaks and feet are suited to where they live and what they eat.

- Many birds migrate. Usually this means going north in spring and summer to feed and nest, and then going south in the winter.

- Mammals share five characteristics: they 1) have hair on their bodies; 2) give birth to live young; 3) feed their young with milk from the mother's breasts; 4) care for their young until they can care for themselves; 5) have big brains.

- There is a great variety of mammals. People belong to a group called primates. People are the smartest animals alive.

Chapter Quiz

Write the answers to the following questions on a separate sheet of paper.

1. Why must birds sit on their eggs?
2. Why are a bird's bones hollow?
3. Why do you think some birds migrate?
4. How do biologists think migrating birds find their way? Can you think of any other ways they might stay on course?
5. Why do hawks have sharp, hooked beaks and claws?
6. Why do ducks have webbed feet?
7. How do biologists know that whales are mammals and not fish?
8. What is unusual about kangaroos as mammals?
9. Why do meat-eating mammals need good eyesight and great speed?
10. What is the largest group of mammals? Name four kinds of animals in this group.

Why Can Birds Fly?

On a separate sheet of paper, list the characteristics of a bird's body that make it possible for the bird to fly. Think of at least four.

Mad Scientist Challenge: Comparing Birds and Mammals

Birds and mammals have several things in common. Think of as many shared features as you can. On a separate sheet of paper, write them in a paragraph. Begin your paragraph with a good topic sentence. A topic sentence tells what the paragraph is about.

Unit 4 Review

Answer the following questions on a separate sheet of paper.

1. How does a sponge get its food?

2. How do earthworms move?

3. What are the three characteristics of arthropods?

4. What are the three parts of an insect's body?

5. What is an amphibian?

6. How do frogs reproduce?

7. How do snakes eat?

8. Why do birds sit on their eggs?

9. Why are whales and dolphins not classified as fish?

10. How do mammals feed their young?

Humans: The Big Brain Mammals

Chapter 15

The Sense Organs

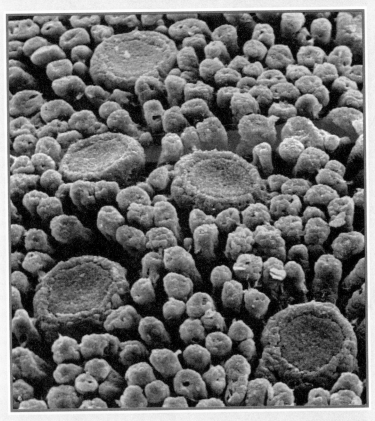

This is the surface of a tongue magnified 240 times. The larger circular features you see are taste buds.

Chapter Learning Objectives

- Name the five senses and their organs.
- Describe the jobs of the skin, eyes, ears, tongue, and nose.
- Explain the relationship between the brain and the sense organs.

Words to Know

dermis a thick layer of skin, under the epidermis, which contains nerves, hair roots, blood vessels, and sweat and oil glands

eardrum the tightly stretched membrane inside the ear that is sensitive to sound

epidermis the outermost layer of skin

iris the colored part of the eye surrounding the pupil

pupil the black circle in the center of the eye

receptor cells body cells that receive outside information

retina the light-sensitive layer of receptor cells at the back of the eyeball

taste buds receptor cells on the tongue that are sensitive to taste

---

People enjoy tasting food, listening to music, touching things, smelling flowers, and watching movies. All of these activities are possible because of five important organs: skin, eyes, ears, tongue, and nose.

But these organs do more than help you enjoy the world. They send very important information to your brain every second. In this chapter, you will learn how each organ gathers information from the world around you.

Have you ever heard something and looked for the source of the sound without thinking? What does this mean?

What Are the Five Senses?

People get information about the world through their senses. The five senses are touch, sight, hearing, taste, and smell.

Each sense is controlled by a special organ. Skin controls the sense of touch. Eyes control the sense of sight. Ears control the sense of hearing. The tongue controls the sense of taste. And the nose controls the sense of smell.

These sense organs collect information. This information is taken in by **receptor cells**. Then it is passed along by nerve cells to the brain. The brain decides what to do with the information. This figuring out what something means is called *interpreting*. The sensory receptors, nerve cells, and brain cells work very fast. The whole process of collecting and interpreting information happens instantly.

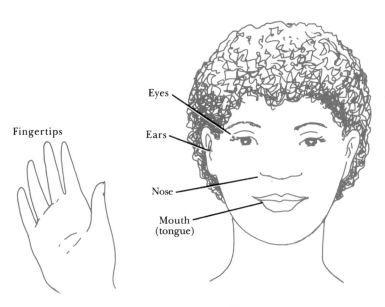

The sense organs

Skin and Touch

The skin is the largest human organ. It covers the whole body. Skin is very thin on the eyelids. It is thickest on the bottom of your feet.

Skin has four important jobs. One, it keeps harmful bacteria out of your body. Two, it keeps the water in your body from drying up. The outer layer of skin is waterproof. And oil glands in the skin produce oils that keep the skin moist. Three, skin regulates the temperature of your body. Layers of fat in the skin help to keep you warm. Sweat glands in the skin let the body give off moisture through the skin. This helps you cool off. Four, skin is the sense organ of touch.

Think of the skin as your body's first line of defense.

Amazing Biology

All organisms must avoid drying out. Eggs help young birds. Scales help reptiles. Amphibians and fish must live in water or they would dry out. All organisms need water. So all organisms must have ways to keep their bodies moist.

The skin is especially sensitive to heat, cold, pressure, and pain. Some parts of your skin are more sensitive than others. Your fingers have many more receptor cells than your arms. Your skin feels texture when something presses against it. Texture is the nature of the pressure on the skin. Something smooth presses one way. Something rough presses another way.

The outer layer of skin is called the **epidermis**. It is mostly made up of dead cells. Millions of these cells come off you every day. The next layer of skin is called the **dermis**. This is a thick layer. It contains blood vessels, nerves, hair roots, oil glands, and sweat glands. Hair, fingernails, and toenails are made of dead skin cells. They grow out of live cells.

Biology Alert

Have you ever had your "hair stand on end" during a scary movie? That is caused by tiny muscles at the roots of your hairs. These muscles flex all at once and cause your head to feel prickly.

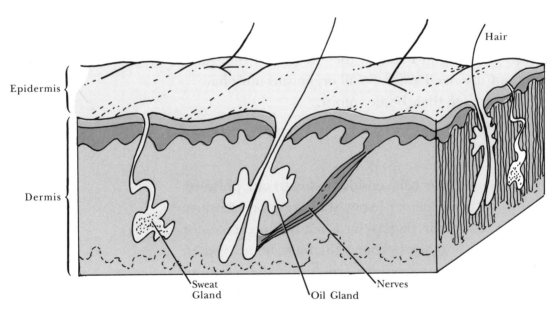

The skin is the largest human organ.

On the Cutting Edge

Doctors are learning more about skin all the time. Recent research has shown that too much suntanning can be bad for skin. It causes skin to age and wrinkle sooner. Worse, repeated sunburns can lead to skin cancer.

Doctors are also learning more and more about how to treat skin burns. With very bad burns, the damaged skin must be removed. New skin is patched over the open place. This is called *skin-grafting*. New skin can be gotten from a skin bank. A skin bank is a place where samples of skin are preserved for emergencies.

Usually the burned person's body rejects the new skin. But special drugs help to keep the skin in place for several weeks. In that time, the burned person can begin growing his or her own new skin.

Eyes and Sight

Everything you see is light. Suppose you are looking at a car. Light bounces off the car and enters your eye. Receptor cells pick up the light. The "light information" is sent to your brain. There it is interpreted. Then you know you are seeing a car.

Light enters the eye through the **pupil**. This is the black opening in the center of your eye. The pupil is surrounded by the colored part of your eye called the **iris**. There are muscles in the iris. These open and close the pupil. When you are in bright light, the muscles close. They make the pupil very small so that just a little light enters. When you are in the dark, the muscles open up wide. This allows more light to enter the pupil so that you can see.

Once light enters your eye, it hits the **retina**. This is the layer of receptor cells at the back of your eye. The retina is like the film in a camera.

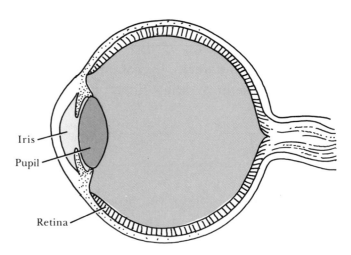

Iris

Pupil

Retina

The eye collects light.

The retina is attached to a thick group of nerve cells. These nerves carry the light messages to your brain. Your brain makes sense of the messages and you see a picture. The picture you see is really in your brain, not your eye. Your eye only collects light.

Eyelids, eyebrows, eyelashes, and tears all protect your eyes. Tears come from a gland above each eye. Tears wash dust and other particles out of the eyes. They also have a substance that kills bacteria.

Biology Practice

Write the main job or jobs of each item listed below. Work on a separate sheet of paper.

1. skin   2. iris   3. pupil   4. tears

Ears and Sound

Sound moves in waves. The sound waves are made by particles bumping into one another. The sound waves travel through the air to reach your ear. Sound can also travel through water.

Sound travels five times faster through seawater than through air.

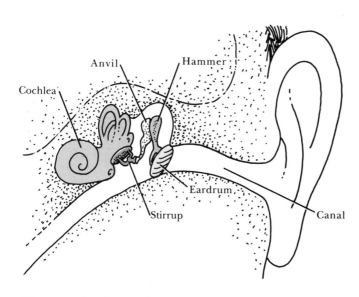

The ear picks up sound waves.

Your ears pick up sound waves. These waves pass inside the ear to the **eardrum**. The eardrum is a membrane. When sound waves hit this membrane, the eardrum vibrates. There are three tiny bones attached to the eardrum. They are called the *hammer bone*, the *anvil bone,* and the *stirrup bone.* These bones pick up the vibrations from the eardrum. In the innermost part of the ear is a snail-shaped organ called the *cochlea.* It has a liquid and tiny hairs inside. The liquid picks up the vibrations and passes them to the tiny hairs. These tiny hairs are nerve endings. They pass the sound waves to nerves attached to the brain. The brain interprets the message as sound.

Amazing Biology

Your sense organs miss a lot. Your eyes can only see a little of the light in the world. The same is true for sound. Sound waves are measured in vibrations. Humans can hear sound waves moving anywhere from 30 to 20,000 vibrations per second. Dogs can hear up to 25,000 or 30,000 vibrations per second. Bats can hear up to 150,000 vibrations per second. In fact, humans are blind and deaf to most of the energy in the world.

The Tongue and Taste

Your tongue is covered with receptor cells that are sensitive to taste. These are called **taste buds**. You have four kinds of taste buds. Some taste sour things, some taste sweet things, some taste salty things, and some taste bitter things. The "tongue map" on this page shows where each of these kinds of taste buds are located.

The Nose and Smell

Much of what you believe to be taste is really smell. As you eat, vapors from your food enter your nose. If you don't believe this, think about eating when you have a head cold. It is hard to taste the food. That is because your nose is stuffed up. You are not *smelling* the food.

Smells are picked up by receptors in the nose. These cells have long, hair-like cilia. The cilia are connected to nerves. Once they pick up a smell, they pass it along. The nerves carry the smell message to the brain. The brain interprets the smell.

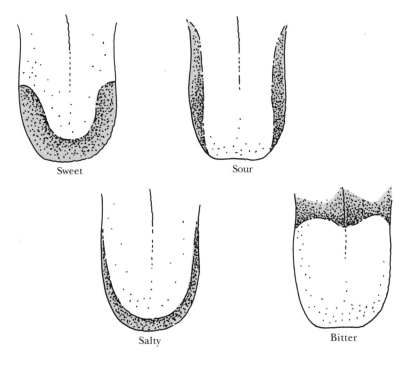

Sweet

Sour

Salty

Bitter

The tongue is covered with four kinds of taste buds.

Chapter Review

Chapter Summary

- The sense organs collect information about the world. Nerves carry this information to the brain. The brain interprets the information.

- Touch, sight, hearing, taste, and smell are the five senses. Skin, eyes, ears, the tongue, and the nose are the five sense organs.

- Skin has four jobs. It keeps harmful bacteria out. It keeps the body from drying out. It regulates body temperature. And it is the sense organ of touch. The outer layer of skin is called the epidermis. The inner layer is called the dermis.

- The eyes take in light through the pupil. The light is received by cells on the retina at the back of the eye. Nerve cells carry this light information to the brain. There it is interpreted as a picture.

- Sound waves are vibrations in the air or water. These are collected by your outer ear. These vibrations move inside your ear to your eardrum. From there the vibrations are passed along to other parts in your inner ear. Finally, they reach tiny hairs that are connected to nerves. The nerves carry the message to the brain. The brain interprets the message as sound.

- The tongue is the organ of taste. Taste buds on the tongue can pick up four different flavors: bitter, sweet, salty, and sour.

- The nose is the organ of smell. Cilia inside the nose are connected to nerves. The nerves carry the smell message to the brain.

Chapter Quiz

Write the answers to the following questions on a separate sheet of paper.

1. Name the five senses and their organs.
2. Which human organ interprets all the information taken in by the senses?
3. What might happen to people if their skin did not have oils in it?
4. What is the outer layer of skin called?
5. Where does light enter the eye? How does enough light enter so that people can see at night?
6. What protects the eye?
7. What does the eardrum do?
8. What four flavors can the tongue taste?
9. What are the receptor cells in the nose like?
10. Which of the sense organs is the largest?

Writing a Study Outline

On a separate sheet of paper, make a study outline of this chapter. Use the headings below. Under each heading, write two or three important details.

THE SENSE ORGANS

1. Skin
2. Eyes
3. Ears
4. Tongue
5. Nose

Mad Scientist Challenge: Five Senses

Write a paragraph on a separate sheet of paper. Describe a person who is using all five senses. Tell what information he or she receives from each of the senses.

Chapter 16

Food: Nutrition and Digestion

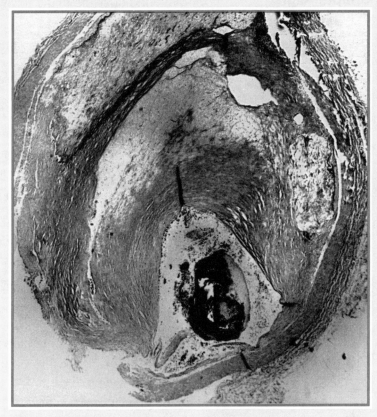

This is a greatly enlarged view of a human coronary artery. It shows that the flow of blood is partly cut off by cholesterol buildup.

Chapter Learning Objectives

- List the six nutrients the body needs.
- Name the main organs of the digestive system.
- Describe what happens to food as it moves through the digestive system.

Words to Know

calorie   the basic unit of food energy

cellulose   a kind of carbohydrate that people cannot digest

cholesterol   a waxy substance made by the body and also found in fatty foods

digestion   the process by which the body breaks food down into nutrients that can be absorbed by the cells

enzyme   a substance that causes chemicals to change form in the body

esophagus   a tube behind the windpipe that carries food from the mouth to the stomach

minerals   non-living substances found in small amounts in certain foods

proteins   nutrients in foods that build body tissues

saliva   a liquid in the mouth that aids digestion

villi   (singular, villus) tiny finger-shaped structures in the walls of the small intestine that absorb digested food into the blood

vitamins   living substances found in certain foods that the body needs to function properly and to resist diseases

Your body is about two-thirds water. If you lost just ten percent of that water, you would become quite sick. If you lost twenty percent of that water, you would probably die.

In order to stay healthy, you must drink a sufficient amount of water each day. Besides water, your body needs food. After all, you are not a plant. You cannot carry out photosynthesis to make your own food. In this chapter you will learn how much water and what kinds of foods your body needs. You will also learn how your body makes use of food.

What Is Nutrition?

What do you think about when you bite into a burrito? Or a hamburger? Or a peach? You probably think about how great it tastes. Most likely you are *not* thinking about how your food is going to get into your bloodstream. Somehow, though, that burrito has to get broken down into simple substances to feed your cells. Those simple substances are called nutrients.

Nutrients are the food molecules that each of your body cells needs. They are used for growth, repair, and energy. To be strong and healthy, you must get six kinds of nutrients: water, minerals, vitamins, proteins, carbohydrates, and fats.

Nutrients are often measured in calories. A **calorie** is a measure of food energy. One calorie of food will give you a certain amount of energy. People who want to gain weight try to eat more calories. People who want to lose weight eat fewer calories. Appendix G at the back of the book shows the number of calories in certain foods.

Plants make starches from simple sugar. When you eat a potato, or a carrot, your body must break it down into simple sugars again to feed your cells.

Biology Alert

Dieting can be dangerous to your health. Studies show that most people gain back the weight they lose on diets, especially if they lose the weight quickly. The smart way to stay in shape is to get plenty of exercise. At the same time, eat healthy foods — but don't make yourself go hungry!

Water

Every cell in your body needs water to do its work. Water aids your body's chemical reactions. It helps get rid of wastes. And it keeps your body at the right temperature. Drinking lots of water cleanses your body. It helps to keep many different sicknesses away. You should drink from six to eight glasses of water a day.

What about sodas, juices, coffee, tea, or milk? Can these count as glasses of water each day? That depends. Coffee, tea, and some sodas have caffeine in them. They also contain some sugar. They have many chemicals that are not good for you. If you drink sodas, coffee, or tea, it is best to drink them *in addition* to water. Natural juices and milk are full of nutrients. They can count for your glasses of water a day.

Minerals

Minerals are nonliving substances. Zinc, iron, calcium, and phosphorus are all minerals needed by your body. Most people think of these minerals as substances found in metals and rocks. They are. But they are also found in small amounts in foods. These minerals give strength to the body tissues. Appendix I at the back of the book lists the minerals your body needs. It also tells which foods contain the minerals, and what each mineral does for your body.

Vitamins

Vitamins are living molecules that your body cannot make enough of by itself. Vitamins aid growth. They also take part in the chemical processes that go on in the body. Dairy products, grains, eggs, fruits, and vegetables are all very high in vitamins. Appendix H at the back of the book lists the vitamins your body needs. It tells which foods contain the vitamins, and what each vitamin does for your body.

Biology Alert

Should you take extra vitamins? Some people believe that if you eat well, you will get all the vitamins you need. Others believe that it is a good idea to take extra vitamins.

But too much of certain vitamins can be quite harmful. For example, Vitamin A is important. Without it, a person will not grow well. Night blindness and bad teeth may also result. But *too much* Vitamin A can cause weak bones. It can cause hair to fall out. If you have questions about how much of a vitamin to take, ask a doctor or nurse.

Proteins

Proteins are used by the body for growth and healing. Your muscles, bones, skin, hair, and nails are all made from proteins. Meats, fish, eggs, dairy products, grains, beans, and nuts all have lots of protein.

Proteins are very active. They perform a wide variety of chemical tasks in your body. Proteins are important to your ability to move. Muscle tissue is mostly protein. Proteins also transport many other materials through the circulatory system. Proteins are large, heavy molecules. They play a major role in holding your body together.

Proteins

Carbohydrates

Carbohydrates are used by the body for energy. Starches, such as potatoes and pasta, are a good source of carbohydrates. Grains, cereals, beans, fruits, and vegetables are other good sources.

Carbohydrates are the sugars that plants make. This sugar is stored as starch in leaves, roots, stems, and fruits. Plants produce another kind of carbohydrate called **cellulose**. Although people cannot digest cellulose, it is a very good thing to eat. Cellulose puts *fiber* in our food. Fiber is a material in food that passes through the digestive system and cleans it out. The cellulose helps clean out the waste in our digestive systems.

Carbohydrates

Fats

The body needs some fat for energy and to cushion the internal organs. However, most people get too much fat in their food. This extra fat can build up on the inside of blood vessels, making it hard for the blood to flow through them properly. Sometimes a blood vessel gets blocked. A blockage in the heart can cause a heart attack. A blockage in the brain can cause a stroke.

Fatty foods include butter, margarine, cooking oil, sausage, bacon, fried foods, lard, nuts, beef, pork, potato chips, corn chips, and cream. It is a good idea to eat as few of these foods as you can. It's healthier to choose meat with less fat, such as fish or chicken.

It is not healthy to eat too many fatty foods.

On the Cutting Edge

Many new studies have come out about **cholesterol**. This is a waxy substance that your body makes. Cholesterol is also found in foods such as animal fats, egg yolks, shrimp, and liver.

Cholesterol works with fat. Together they can lead to blockage of blood vessels. Studies show that eating a lot of fat causes your body to make more cholesterol. More and more doctors are suggesting that people cut way back on fatty and cholesterol-rich foods.

Biology Practice

Complete each sentence on a separate sheet of paper.

1. Your body is about two-thirds_____.
2. _____ are the food molecules that each of your body cells need.
3. Minerals are _____ substances.
4. Meat, fish, eggs, beans, and nuts are all good sources of _____.
5. Cellulose helps to clean out the _____ in our digestive systems.

The Five Food Groups

How can you be sure that you get all six nutrients in your diet every day? The chart on this page shows the five food groups. It tells how many daily servings from each food group you should eat. If you follow this chart, you will get enough of the six nutrients.

The Five Food Groups	
Group	**Foods in the Group**
Milk Group 2 to 3 servings a day	Milk, cheese, ice cream, yogurt
Meat, Fish, Nuts Group 2 to 3 servings a day	Beef, pork, chicken, lamb, seafood
Vegetable Group 3 to 5 servings a day	Spinach, carrots, lettuce, cabbage
Fruit Group 2 to 4 servings a day	Oranges, berries, apples, grapes
Bread-Cereal Group 6 to 11 servings a day	Whole grain cereals, macaroni, spaghetti, rice

The Digestive System

Your blood carries nutrients from the food you eat all over your body. Before that can happen, though, the food must be broken down into simple substances. A whole tuna sandwich cannot move through your blood vessels. The process of breaking your food down into nutrients is called **digestion**.

Digestion is carried out by five organs: the mouth, esophagus, stomach, small intestine, and large intestine. These organs are all connected. In fact, they are really just one long tube.

In many of these organs, **enzymes** help with digestion. An enzyme is a substance that causes chemicals to change. Enzymes also speed a chemical reaction. In digestion, enzymes help to break down food quickly.

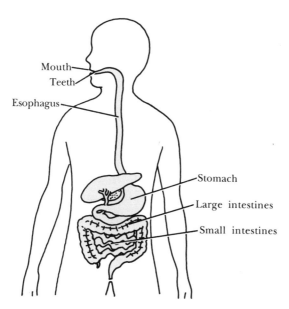

Mouth
Teeth
Esophagus
Stomach
Large intestines
Small intestines

The digestive system

The Mouth and Esophagus

Once you put food into your mouth, your teeth go to work. They bite and chew the food into smaller pieces. You have three kinds of teeth. In the front of your mouth are teeth that bite, called *incisors*. Next to them are teeth that tear, called *canines*. In the back of your mouth are teeth that grind food down, called *molars*. Your teeth chew the food until it is small enough to swallow.

As you chew, a liquid called **saliva** is released. This wets the food and helps you to swallow. Saliva also has an enzyme that breaks starch down into simple sugar.

There are two openings at the back of your mouth. One leads to your lungs. A flap of tissue covers this opening. That keeps food from going down into your lungs. The other opening at the back of your mouth leads to the **esophagus**. The esophagus connects the mouth to the stomach. Muscles in the esophagus push the food down.

The Stomach, Small Intestine, and Large Intestine

Food passes from the esophagus into the stomach. It can be stored there for up to six hours. Muscles in the stomach move the food around. More enzymes are released to break down the food. Acids are also released. These acids are strong enough to dissolve most metals.

When the food leaves the stomach, it goes into the small intestine. This organ is only an inch wide. But it is about 25 feet long! It is tightly coiled up below the

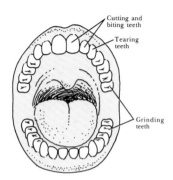

Cutting and biting teeth

Tearing teeth

Grinding teeth

Humans have three kinds of teeth.

Sometimes stomach acids work their way through the lining of the stomach wall. This causes a very painful open sore. It is called an ulcer.

stomach. Most digestion takes place in the small intestine. Here the food is completely broken down into nutrient molecules.

The lining of the small intestine is not smooth. It has many folds and tiny finger-shaped structures called **villi**. The folds and villi increase the surface area of the small intestine many times. More surface area means more nutrients can be absorbed.

The villi are full of tiny blood vessels. They absorb the nutrient molecules into the bloodstream. Blood carries the nutrients to all parts of the body.

Every bit of the food you eat cannot be digested. These leftovers pass into the large intestine. The large intestine absorbs water out of the wastes. Then the wastes pass out of the body.

People in Biology: Lynn Margulis

Lynn Margulis, a cell biologist, found that cells, including all the cells in the human body, are derived from bacteria. Remember that bacteria are tiny, very simple living things that do not have nuclei in their cells. Our bodies are made up of 10 billion animal cells and *100* billion bacteria cells. In fact, lots of bacteria live in parts of your digestive system. These bacteria help to break down your food.

Margulis believes that if you killed off all the bacteria on Earth, the planet would be just as bare and rocky as the moon within weeks.

Chapter Review

Chapter Summary

- Nutrients are the molecules of food and water all your body cells need. There are six main nutrients: water, minerals, vitamins, carbohydrates, proteins, and fats. The best way to get all six nutrients daily is to eat from all four food groups.

- Every cell in your body needs water. Water aids your body's chemical reactions and helps it get rid of wastes.

- Vitamins are living molecules that your body cannot make enough of by itself. Vitamins aid growth and take part in the chemical processes in your body.

- The body uses proteins for growth and healing. The body uses carbohydrates for energy.

- Fats are a problem food. The body needs some fat for energy and to cushion the internal organs. But most people have too much fat in their food.

- Digestion is carried out by five organs: the mouth, esophagus, stomach, small intestine, and large intestine. The digestive process begins when you take a bite of food. After the food is chewed, enzymes break down starches into sugar. The food passes down the esophagus into the stomach, where acids break it down further. Then it passes into the small intestine where the food continues to be digested. Nutrients pass through the villi into the bloodstream.

- Your body cannot digest all the food it eats. Wastes pass into the large intestine and out of the body.

Chapter Quiz

Write the answers to the following questions on a separate sheet of paper.

1. What must happen to a tuna sandwich before your body cells can use it?
2. Name the six nutrients needed by your body.
3. Why do you need to drink enough water every day?
4. Which of the six nutrients are non-living substances?
5. In what ways do your body cells use protein?
6. Explain why eating too much fat can be dangerous.
7. Which foods have cholesterol in them?
8. How does food get down the esophagus?
9. In which organ is food absorbed into the bloodstream?
10. How do teeth help in digestion?

The Digestive System

Make a copy of the chart below on a separate sheet of paper. Then fill in the boxes.

The Five Organs of the Digestive System	
Organ	**Its Main Job**

Mad Scientist Challenge: The Five Food Groups

On a separate sheet of paper, plan a menu for one day. Include breakfast, lunch, and dinner. Plan your meals using the recommended servings of the five food groups. Make sure the menu provides the six nutrients a person needs.

Chapter 17

Movement: Bones and Muscles

This photograph of the heart shows the opening to the pulmonary artery. The heart is the hardest-working muscle in the body.

Chapter Learning Objectives

- Name the four jobs of the skeleton.
- Describe what bones are made of.
- Describe the three kinds of muscle.

Words to Know

cardiac muscle   the muscle tissue that makes up the heart

involuntary muscle   a muscle that moves automatically, without your thinking about it

joints   the places in the body where two or more bones are joined, usually in a way that allows them to move

ligaments   bands of tissue that hold bones together

marrow   the soft center of bones where red blood cells are made

tendons   bands of tissue that attach muscles to bones

voluntary muscle   a muscle that moves when you decide to move it

You have 206 bones in your body. All these bones combine to make up your skeleton. Without a skeleton of bones, you would not be able to stand up. You would be a soft bag of skin and organs. Your head would be soft and mushy.

This chapter is about bones and muscles, the body systems that support and move you.

The Skeletal System

Your bones have four jobs. One, they provide a frame for your body. Two, they protect many organs inside your body. Your brain, for example, is protected by the bones that make up your *skull.* Your rib bones form a cage around the heart and lungs. Three, bones work with muscles for body movement. Many of the muscles in your body are attached to bones. Four, some bones even make blood cells. These blood cells are made in the soft center of bones. This soft center where red blood cells are made is called the **marrow.**

You are a vertebrate. That means you have a backbone. Since your backbone is vertical, you walk upright.

The largest bone in your body is the thigh bone. The smallest bone is in your ear.

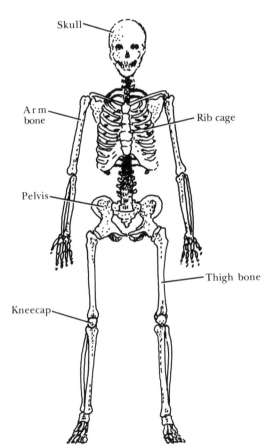

The skeletal system

What Are Bones Made Of?

Bones are made of both living and non-living materials. The living materials are bone cells, blood cells, and nerve cells. These cells make up about one-third of bones. About two-thirds of bones are made up of non-living materials. The minerals calcium and phosphorous make bones hard. If your bones did not have these minerals, they would be too soft to support you.

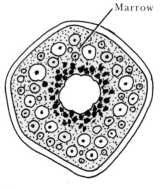

Cross section of bone

A few months before you were born, your whole skeleton was made of *cartilage*. This is the material that makes your nose and ears able to bend. Cartilage is much like bone. The difference is that cartilage does not have the minerals calcium and phosphorus in it.

These minerals build up in bones as people grow older. They make the bones much more brittle. That is why older people break bones more easily than younger people.

Broken bones can grow back together and heal. The part of a bone that is living is made of cells that reproduce. These cells form new bone tissue to heal a broken bone. To help the healing process, a doctor usually sets a broken bone in a cast. This holds the bone still so it will heal correctly.

Bone Joints

Bones are held together by strong bands of tissue called **ligaments**. The places where two bones meet are called **joints**.

There are several kinds of joints. The skull is an example of an *immovable joint*. The bones there meet in what look like cracks. These bones do not move.

Your hip and shoulder joints are examples of *ball-and-socket joints*. These allow bones to move in almost any direction. You can even swing your arm or leg in a circle.

Now try swinging the end of your arm—from your elbow—in a circle. You cannot do it. That's because the joint at your elbow is a *hinge joint*. It can only move in one direction—up and down. Your knees, toes, and fingers also have hinge joints.

There are *gliding joints* in your neck and wrists. These joints allow bones to glide over one another. You use these joints when you open a jar.

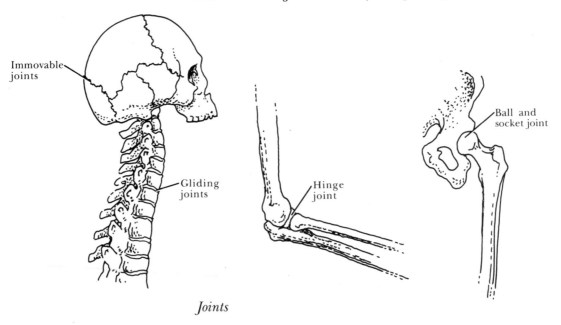

Immovable joints

Gliding joints

Hinge joint

Ball and socket joint

Joints

Biology Practice

Write the answers to the following questions on a separate sheet of paper.

1. Name two jobs of bones.
2. Where are red blood cells made?
3. What are bones made of?
4. Name two hinge joints in your body.

On the Cutting Edge

Sports medicine is a growing field. More and more Americans are becoming interested in fitness. Unfortunately, this means there are more and more sports injuries.

Good athletes always follow a few simple precautions. They always warm up well. This means taking time to stretch out muscles before beginning a hard work-out. It also means starting out slowly. Warming up prevents an athlete from pulling muscles.

Knowing your limits is another good idea. If you have never run more than a quarter mile, do not set out to run five miles. Work toward your goal slowly. Injuries often happen when people push their limits too far or too fast.

Using the right equipment will also protect you against injury. For example, if you are a skier, well-fitting boots may save a leg.

There are several interesting jobs in sports medicine. Doctors, nurses, physical therapists, and trainers all work in sports clinics.

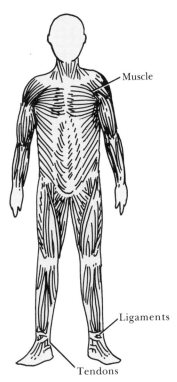

The muscular system

Muscles

Your bones cannot move on their own. They move because they are attached to muscles. **Tendons** hold muscles onto bones. Your body has about 700 muscles. Almost half your weight is muscle.

There are three kinds of muscle tissue in your body. The muscles attached to your bones are called *skeletal muscles*. These are **voluntary muscles**. You decide when to move them. A voluntary muscle moves your skeleton by pulling on the tendon. The muscles you use for chewing, throwing, kicking, lifting, and talking are all voluntary.

The second kind of muscle tissue is called *smooth muscle*. These are **involuntary muscles**. They work whether you want them to or not. They work even while you are sleeping. Smooth muscles are found in the walls of your stomach and intestines. They help move food through your digestive system. They are also found in blood vessels where they help move blood along. Smooth muscles are not attached to bones.

The third kind of muscle tissue is called **cardiac muscle**. Cardiac muscle is a type of involuntary muscle only found in your heart. Cardiac muscle works all the time—your heart is always beating. Cardiac muscle is the strongest muscle tissue in the body. Your heart is the hardest working muscle in your body.

How Muscles Work

Muscles move when they get orders from the brain. These orders travel along nerve cells. When a muscle does move, it contracts, or shortens. When the nerve message stops, it relaxes, or lengthens.

Muscles can only pull. They cannot push. For this reason, muscles work in pairs. One muscle extends a limb. This is called the *extensor*. The other muscle bends the limb at the joint. This is called a *flexor*. The extensor and the flexor oppose each other. So they are called an *antagonistic pair*. When one of the muscles contracts, the other relaxes.

Try holding your arm out straight. Now, bend your elbow. You will see a bulge in your upper arm. This is the *bicep*. The bicep is a flexor muscle. Now straighten your arm. The bicep relaxes. As your arm straightens, your *tricep* bulges. The tricep is an extensor muscle. Working together, the bicep and tricep allow you to lift and lower things.

The opposing muscles balance each other. This balance allows you to move smoothly and efficiently.

Amazing Biology

Some people face a big surprise when they begin working out and getting in shape. Though they exercise more, they gain weight! This happens because muscle weighs more than fat. If you lose some fat and gain some muscle, you will gain weight.

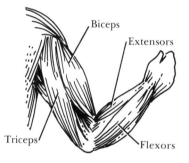

Arm muscles

Chapter Review

Chapter Summary

- There are 206 bones in the human skeleton. These bones have four jobs: 1) they are a frame for the body; 2) they protect organs inside the body; 3) they work with muscles for body movement; 4) they help to make red blood cells.

- About one-third of bone matter is made up of living cells: bone cells, blood cells, and nerve cells. About two-thirds of bone matter is made up of non-living minerals: calcium and phosphorous. These minerals make bones hard.

- The places where bones meet are called joints. Ligaments hold bones together at the joint. There are several kinds of joints. Immovable joints do not move. Ball-and-socket joints allow bones to move in almost any direction, including in a circle. Hinge joints allow bones to move up and down. Gliding joints allow bones to slide over one another.

- Tendons attach muscles to bones. There are three kinds of muscles. Skeletal muscles are attached to bone. They are voluntary muscles. They move when a person decides to move them. Smooth muscles are involuntary muscles. They move automatically without a person thinking about it. They are found in the stomach, intestines, and blood vessels. Cardiac muscle is a special type of involuntary muscle found only in the heart.

- Muscles can pull, but they cannot push. For that reason, muscles work in pairs. That allows them to move the body smoothly in different directions.

Chapter Quiz

Write the answers to the following questions on a separate sheet of paper.

1. How many bones are there in your body?

2. What kind of joints are in your skull?

3. Where are red blood cells made?

4. What minerals are found in bone? What do these minerals do for your bones?

5. What kind of joint is in your shoulder?

6. What kind of joints allow you to bend your fingers?

7. Give two examples of involuntary muscles.

8. Which kind of muscles move the bones of your skeleton?

9. Why do muscles work in pairs?

10. What is the difference between ligaments and tendons?

Bones or Muscles?

Decide whether each sentence below is about bones or muscles. Write your answer on a separate sheet of paper.

1. There are 206 of them in your body.

2. They protect your brain, heart, and lungs.

3. Some are voluntary and others involuntary.

4. There are about 700 of them in your body.

5. They make up about half of your weight.

6. Red blood cells are made in them.

7. They are made of both living and non-living tissue.

8. Your heart is made of it.

Mad Scientist Challenge: Reporting on the Skeleton

Write a report on a separate sheet of paper. In your own words, describe the four jobs of the skeleton. Try to give one example for each job.

Chapter 18

Life Support: Oxygen and Blood

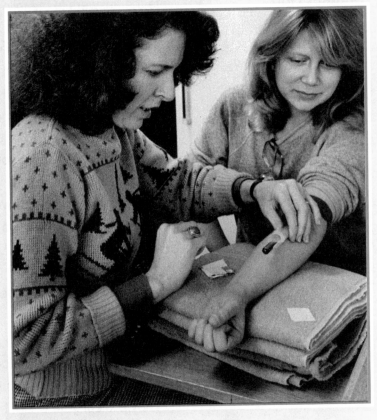

Have you ever had your blood tested? By testing blood, doctors can check for a variety of diseases. And they can learn about the condition of most of the organs and tissues in the body.

Chapter Learning Objectives

- Describe the parts and function of the circulatory system.
- Describe the parts and function of the respiratory system.
- List two ways to keep the circulatory and respiratory systems healthy.

Words to Know

arteries   blood vessels that carry blood away from the heart

atria   the upper chambers of the heart

capillaries   tiny blood vessels through which nutrients, oxygen, and wastes are exchanged with body cells and air sacs in the lungs

coronary system   the part of the circulatory system that supplies oxygen to the heart

plasma   the liquid part of blood

platelets   solids in blood plasma that help to make blood clot

veins   blood vessels that carry blood toward the heart

ventricles   the lower chambers of the heart

Put your hand in the middle of your chest. There you will find your heart, the hardest working organ in your body. It beats between 60 and 80 times a minute. Every day it pumps a dozen pints of blood. This workhorse is only about the size of a large fist.

Your body has about 60 trillion cells. Each one of those cells needs nutrients and oxygen. Each one also needs to get rid of wastes. In this chapter you will learn how your body cells get what they need for energy.

Your heart pumps blood steadily even when you are asleep.

What Is the Circulatory System?

Blood flows throughout your body. This blood carries oxygen and nutrients to all your body cells. It carries wastes away from the body cells. The flow of blood in your body makes up the *circulatory system*. It is the transportation system for the blood cells in your body.

The circulatory system is made up of blood, the heart, and blood vessels. Blood vessels are the tubes through which blood flows. There are 60,000 miles of blood vessels coiled up in your body.

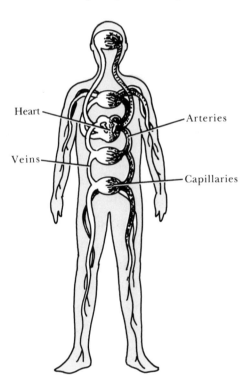

The circulatory system

Remember that nutrients are food that has been broken down into molecules by the digestive system.

The Heart and the Flow of Blood

The heart is the engine of the circulatory system. It pumps to keep the blood flowing throughout the body. The heart is a big muscle that weighs about ten ounces. It is divided into four parts called chambers. The two top chambers are called **atria**. The two bottom chambers are called **ventricles**.

Veins are blood vessels that carry blood *toward* the heart. **Arteries** are blood vessels that carry blood *away* from the heart.

The picture on this page shows the path of blood. First it flows into the right atrium. From there it flows down into the right ventricle. An artery carries the blood out to the lungs. There the blood picks up oxygen. Now the oxygen-rich blood returns to the left atrium. The heart pumps the blood down into the left ventricle. From there it is pumped down into the body. And it travels to every cell delivering nutrients and oxygen.

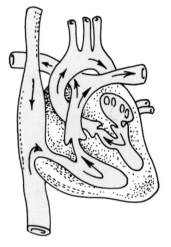

The heart

Biology Alert

Your heart is made of cells. So your heart must have a constant supply of oxygen. A special part of the circulatory system supplies oxygen to the heart. It is called the **coronary system**.

The coronary system is under a great deal of stress. It must supply your heart with oxygen all the time. Most people who have heart problems have weak coronary systems.

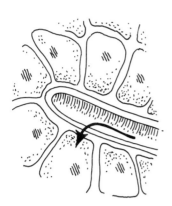

Capillaries

Since the cell wastes are from respiration, they are mostly carbon dioxide and water.

How do the nutrients and oxygen get from the blood into body cells? At the ends of veins and arteries are tiny blood vessels called **capillaries**. These blood vessels are only one cell thick. Oxygen and nutrient molecules can pass through capillaries into the body cells.

At the same time, wastes from the body cells move into the blood at the capillaries. These wastes travel in veins all the way back to the heart. From there they are pumped into the lungs. You exhale the wastes out into the air.

The circulatory system adjusts to meet your body's needs. When you exercise, more blood flows to the muscles of your limbs. When you eat, more blood flows to the muscles of your digestive system.

Taking Care of Your Heart

Blood pressure is measured by how hard flowing blood pushes against the walls of arteries. High blood pressure means the blood must push very hard to get through.

With exercise, the heart pumps lots of blood through blood vessels. This keeps them wide open and elastic. This lessens the chance of a vessel being blocked.

Fats can build up in the arteries. This makes the heart work harder to pump blood. People who want a healthy heart don't smoke or eat too many fats. They exercise and get lots of sleep.

People in Biology: Quang T. Le

Quang T. Le was a medical student when his father developed high blood pressure. His father tried an old Oriental cure: celery. Le's father ate a quarter pound of celery every day for a week. He did not change anything else in his diet. His blood pressure dropped back down to normal.

Quang T. Le and William J. Elliott decided to find out why the celery worked. They discovered that celery contains a chemical that relaxes the smooth-muscle lining of blood vessels. When the lining relaxes, the blood vessels get wider. So the blood flows more easily and blood pressure goes down.

On the Cutting Edge

Some people have a heart condition that makes the heart stop pumping for a moment or two. Without blood going to the brain, a person can die in a matter of minutes.

A tiny device has been invented for people with this heart condition. The device is implanted in the body. It keeps track of the heart. If the heart stops pumping, the device gives a little electrical shock. This shock sets the heart to pumping again.

Biology Practice

On a separate sheet of paper, write T for each sentence that is true and F for each sentence that is false.

1. The circulatory system breaks food down into nutrients.
2. The heart is divided into four chambers.
3. Blood picks up oxygen in the lungs.
4. Fatty foods help to keep the circulatory system healthy.
5. Capillaries are very large blood vessels.

What Is Blood?

You have about one pint of blood for every twelve pounds of body weight. Nine-tenths of this blood is a liquid called **plasma**. Plasma carries the nutrients and wastes through your circulatory system.

There are three kinds of solids in blood: **platelets**, red blood cells, and white blood cells. Platelets are actually pieces of cells. Platelets are used to stop bleeding. They help blood to clot. If it were not for platelets, wounds would never stop bleeding.

Blood has two major functions. The first is to transport nutrients to all the other cells of the body. The second is to fight infection.

Red blood cells deliver nutrients to the other cells of the body. Red blood cells are made in the marrow of your bones. The cells live about four months.

White blood cells fight infection. They destroy harmful bacteria. You have many fewer white blood cells than red blood cells. There is about one white blood cell for every 5,000 red.

Have you ever had a bruise? A bruise is caused by the breaking of small blood vessels under the skin.

Perhaps you have had a wound that formed *pus* around it. This pus is made up of white blood cells that died fighting bacteria.

Biology Alert

Some people suffer from *hemophilia*. This means there are not enough platelets in their blood. So their blood cannot clot. Someone who has hemophilia can lose a great deal of blood from a simple cut.

The Respiratory System

You have studied the process of respiration. This is the way that cells use oxygen and food to get energy. Remember that carbon dioxide and water are waste products of respiration. You now know how body cells get food for respiration. The *respiratory system* provides the necessary oxygen.

Take a deep breath. The air you breathe is full of oxygen. It travels a path in your body. First the air

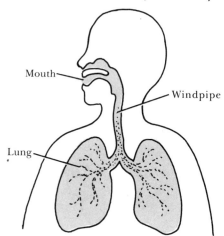

The respiratory system

goes in your nose. The hair and mucus in your nose filter out dust and pollen. This helps to clean the air you breathe. You can also breathe in air through your mouth. But your mouth cannot clean the air as well as your nose can.

Next the breath of air passes over your vocal cords. When you talk, muscles in your throat cause your vocal cords to vibrate. This makes the air you exhale vibrate, creating sound waves in the form of words.

The windpipe carries air from your mouth into your lungs.

Biology Alert

The *epiglottis* is a flap of skin in the back of your mouth that prevents food from going down your windpipe. Sometimes, though, food does go down the windpipe. This makes a person choke. A choking person usually begins coughing automatically. Coughing forces air up from the lungs. This blows the food out of the windpipe.

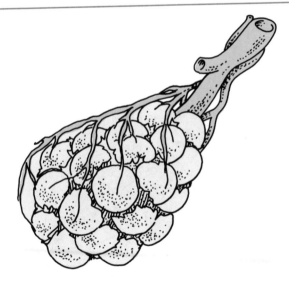

Air sacs in the lungs

Your lungs are big spongy organs. They are filled with branching tubes. The tubes end with millions of tiny air sacs. These air sacs look like bunches of grapes. Each lung has about 150 million air sacs.

The air sacs are covered with capillaries. And like capillaries, the walls of each air sac are only one cell thick. Oxygen passes from the air sac right into the capillary. Blood vessels carry the oxygen-rich blood all over the body.

At the same time, blood in capillaries passes waste water and carbon dioxide into the air sacs. You breathe these wastes out when you exhale.

How Smoking Can Kill You

Smoking can seriously damage the respiratory system. Tar and nicotine clog the air sacs in the lungs. This keeps oxygen from passing into the blood. It also traps wastes in the lungs. Without oxygen, your cells cannot work.

Clogged lungs also make hard work for the heart. It must pump harder to get oxygen. Smokers have three times the chance of a heart attack as non-smokers. Smokers also risk lung cancer.

Chapter Review

Chapter Summary

- The circulatory system is made up of blood, the heart, and blood vessels. It delivers nutrients and oxygen to every cell in your body.

- The heart pumps blood through the blood vessels. The heart has four chambers. The two upper chambers are called atria. The two lower chambers are called ventricles.

- Blood vessels leaving the heart are called arteries. Veins carry blood back to the heart. Capillaries are tiny blood vessels through which nutrients, oxygen, and wastes are exchanged with body cells.

- Blood is made of plasma, red blood cells, white blood cells, and platelets.

- You can take care of your heart by exercising, not smoking, getting plenty of rest, and eating healthy food.

- The respiratory system delivers oxygen to the blood. First air is breathed in through the mouth or nose. The air travels past the vocal cords and goes down the windpipe. From there the air goes into big spongy organs called lungs. The air fills millions of air sacs in the lungs. These air sacs are only one cell thick. They are covered with capillaries which are also only one cell thick. Oxygen passes from the air sacs into the capillaries. Wastes pass from the blood in the capillaries into the air sacs.

- The tar and nicotine from smoking cigarettes can clog the air sacs in your lungs. Smoking can prevent blood from getting enough oxygen to body cells.

Chapter Quiz

Write the answers to the following questions on a separate sheet of paper.

1. About how many times a minute does the human heart beat?
2. What does blood carry to all the body cells?
3. What does blood carry away from the body cells?
4. What organ keeps blood moving through blood vessels?
5. Describe the difference between arteries and veins.
6. Why does high blood pressure present a danger?
7. Name at least two ways to keep your heart and circulatory system healthy.
8. What do white blood cells do for you?
9. What is the job of the respiratory system?
10. How do you make sounds when you talk?

Fill in the Blank

On a separate sheet of paper, write the word that best completes each sentence.

1. Nine-tenths of blood is a liquid called_____.
2. The lungs contain millions of_____.
3. In the lungs, oxygen passes from the air sacs into the _____.
4. The solids in blood plasma that stop the bleeding of a wound are called_____.

Mad Scientist Challenge: Design a Poster

On a separate sheet of paper, design a poster that shows how to keep the heart and circulatory system healthy. Use your imagination. You may want to focus on just one of the dangers to the heart. Or you may want to show several of the possible problems.

Chapter 19

Body Messengers: Neurons and Hormones

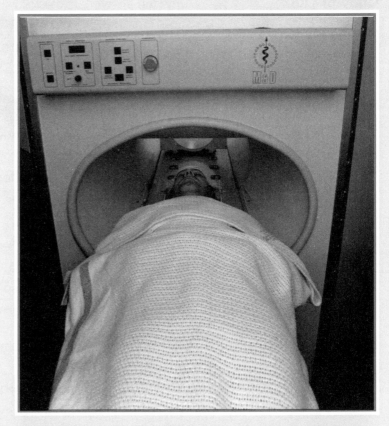

This man is undergoing a brain scan. The reading will show if this man has a brain tumor. Why is the brain such an important part of the body?

Chapter Learning Objectives

- Describe nerves and how they work.
- Describe how the brain controls most activity in the body.
- Explain what hormones do.

Words to Know

adrenaline   a hormone that gives the body extra energy in times of fright, anger, or excitement

axons   the fibers on neurons that carry messages away from the cell

cerebellum   the part of the brain that controls balance and the working together of muscles

cerebrum   the part of the brain that controls voluntary muscle movements, thinking, learning, memory, and the senses

dendrites   the fibers on neurons that carry messages into the cell

hormones   the chemical messengers in the body that are produced by certain glands

medulla   the part of the brain that controls automatic body functions such as involuntary muscle movements

neurons   nerve cells throughout the body that carry signals to and from the brain

reflex   an automatic and involuntary response to an outside stimulus

spinal cord   a rope of neurons that connects the brain and the nervous system

synapses   the spaces between neurons

The human brain weighs about three pounds. This is a very small percent of most people's body weight. Yet the brain uses nearly 25 percent of the energy produced by your body. Thinking burns a lot of energy.

Even when you sleep, your brain is very active. It controls your breathing and heartbeat.

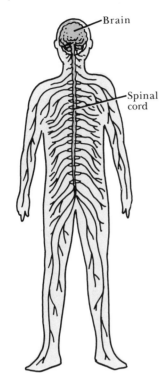

Brain

Spinal cord

The nervous system

The spinal cord connects the nervous system to your brain. The combination of the brain and the spinal cord is called the central nervous system.

Your brain is the command center of your body. Without it, your body would not know what to do with itself. But how does the brain tell your body what to do?

In this chapter you will learn how the brain works for you. You will learn how all the organs in your body communicate.

The Nervous System

The nervous system provides communication among the different organs in your body. It is like the body's telephone service. Your brain is the command center.

The nervous system is made up of cells called **neurons**. Neurons are long stringy nerve cells. A single neuron can run from the bottom of the spinal cord down to a toe—about three feet or more.

There are two main centers of the nervous system, the brain and the **spinal cord**. The brain is a huge mass of neurons packed together. The spinal cord is also a mass of nerve cells. These cells form a long rope. The rope of nerves is protected by your backbone. The spinal cord runs from the brain down to the bottom of your back. The spinal cord acts as the nervous system's main switchboard. All the messages between your brain and the rest of your body must travel along the spinal cord.

How Nerves Carry Messages

The brain is in charge of your body. It sends messages telling different body organs what to do. These messages travel along neurons.

A neuron has a cell body with long fibers coming off it. Some of these fibers carry messages *into* the cell body from outside. These are called **dendrites**. Other fibers on neurons carry messages *away from* the cell body. These are called **axons**.

Messages are passed along the chain of neurons. A message passes from the axon of one neuron to the dendrite of the next neuron. The messages move by electrical impulses. But neurons do not actually touch one another. The spaces between neurons are called **synapses.** And the messages must "jump" these gaps. The messages are carried over the synapses by a special chemical process.

Neurons are constantly carrying messages. This information keeps you aware of your environment.

A neuron

Three Kinds of Neurons

There are three kinds of neurons. *Sensory neurons* are attached to your sense organs—eyes, ears, nose, tongue, and skin. They take messages from the sense organs to the *central nervous system*—the brain and spinal cord. The sense receptors in your fingertips, tongue, and other sense organs are really dendrites. These are the long fibers on neurons that carry messages *toward* the nerve cell.

Motor neurons carry messages from the brain to muscles and glands. The muscles and glands respond to the information from the sensory neurons.

A network of nerve fibers extends from the spinal cord to the rest of the body. This network is called the *peripheral nervous system.*

Relay neurons connect sensory neurons and motor neurons. Relay neurons are found in your central nervous system. The relay neurons complete the circuit of the electrical impulses in the nervous system. After a message reaches the central nervous system, relay neurons pass the information to motor neurons. Without relay neurons, your motor neurons could not respond to the impulse of your sensory neurons.

Here is an example of how the three kinds of neurons work together.

Suppose you catch a finger under a heavy box. Sensory neurons pick up a message from your finger. The message says that the finger is feeling pain and pressure. This message travels up sensory neurons to the spinal cord. Now relay neurons pick up the message and deliver it to motor neurons. The motor neurons rush a message to your arm muscles. Your

First, sensory neurons alert you to the environment. Then relay neurons tell the motor neurons. The motor neurons respond. This is called a response circuit.

arm muscles lift the box off the trapped finger. Sometimes these messages can move so fast you save yourself from feeling pain. This ability to respond can often save you from serious injury.

Biology Alert

The spinal cord is very important—and very vulnerable. Many people suffer from back pain. This can mean that the nerves in the spinal cord are being pinched. Pressure on the nerve keeps the nerves from passing along messages properly. If the back problem is not treated, it can affect the working of the lower body. If the nerve becomes damaged, as in an accident, the person may be seriously handicapped.

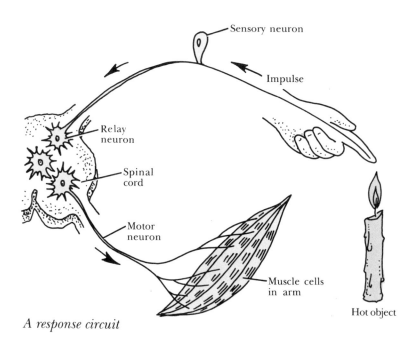

A response circuit

Biology Alert

Alcohol is found in beer, wine, and hard liquor. Alcohol in the body interferes with the nervous system. It slows the messages moving between neurons.

This is why people who drink and drive often get into accidents. Suppose the driver sees a dangerous situation up ahead. The message is taken in by the eyes. It travels very slowly along sensory neurons to the brain. The brain sends back a message along motor neurons. The message is to brake and stop the car. But the message moves so slowly that the driver brakes too late.

Heavy drinking actually kills brain cells. And brain cells do not replace themselves. Lost brain cells are gone forever.

Biology Practice

Write the answers to the following questions on a separate sheet of paper.

1. What type of cells make up the nervous system?
2. What does the spinal cord do?
3. Do axons carry messages to the nerve cell or away from it?
4. What is the central nervous system?
5. What do relay neurons do?

Reflexes and the Spinal Cord

The spinal cord links your brain to the rest of your body. Sometimes it serves as a shortcut for messages that need fast action. Suppose you touch something very hot. A message will race up your hand by sensory neurons. Relay neurons in your spinal cord will send the message to motor neurons in your arm. You will quickly withdraw your hand.

At the same time, relay neurons in the spinal cord will also send a message to the brain. But the message that tells your arm to pull away may arrive first.

Messages that are centered in the spinal cord rather than the brain are called **reflexes**. A reflex is an automatic and involuntary response to an outside stimulus. Reflex actions are not directed by the brain. Many reflexes protect the body from harm.

The process of alert and response in the nervous system is called a reflex arc.

The Brain

More than half of your neurons are packed in your brain. The brain has three main parts. These parts are far more complex than any computer. In fact, the human brain is the most complex thing on Earth. The brain organizes the impulses it receives and responds with impulses to the motor neurons.

The largest part of the brain is the **cerebrum**. The cerebrum has many ridges and folds to create more surface area for cells. The cerebrum controls many voluntary muscle movements. It also controls thinking, learning, and memory. It interprets the messages from sense organs, too.

Voluntary functions, like raising your hand, are things you must control yourself. Involuntary functions, like your heartbeat, are those things you don't think about.

Another part of the brain, the **cerebellum**, is just below the back of the cerebrum. The cerebellum coordinates muscle movements. Working with the cerebrum, it enables you to run, write, and talk. The cerebellum also helps people to keep their balance.

The third part of the brain is the **medulla**. The medulla is the top of the brain stem. The brain stem connects the brain to the spinal cord. The medulla controls automatic body functions. These include breathing, heartbeat, and the involuntary muscles in the digestive system.

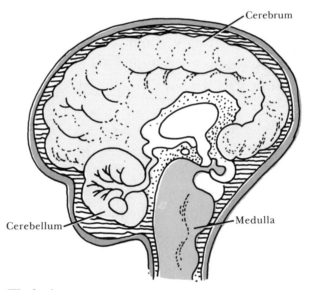

The brain

Another Kind of Messenger: Hormones

Not all body messages are carried by nerves. Some are carried in the bloodstream by chemical substances called **hormones**. These control such things as body growth and behavior. Nerves work by electrical impulses in the nervous system. Hormones work by chemical impulses in the circulatory system.

Hormones are produced by glands. There are several different kinds of hormones produced by different glands throughout the body. Each kind of hormone controls a certain body function.

You may have heard of the hormone **adrenaline**. This hormone is produced by the *adrenal gland*. The adrenal gland goes into action when you become frightened, angry, or excited. This gland causes stored sugar to shoot into the bloodstream. The sugar gives an extra supply of energy to the body cells. Adrenaline also causes the blood to circulate faster. With the extra food and oxygen going to cells, the body suddenly becomes extremely powerful. This explains how people can sometimes perform amazing feats in the face of great danger.

When you are frightened or excited, you may feel a surge of adrenaline in your system.

People in Biology: Candace Pert

Candace Pert is a cutting-edge brain researcher. She studies special messenger chemicals called *peptides*. These are hormones that control communication between the brain and body. People have peptides throughout the body. That's why Pert believes there isn't as much separation between the brain and the rest of the body as some people think.

Pert believes that peptide research will help scientists better understand what causes emotions. She also believes that understanding peptides will lead to treatments for many diseases, including AIDS and cancer.

Chapter Review

Chapter Summary

- The nervous system is made up of neurons. The brain and spinal cord make up the central nervous system. The brain controls most activity in the body. The spinal cord acts as the body's switchboard. It joins the brain to the rest of the body.

- Messages travel from the brain or spinal cord to all parts of the body. These messages are electrical impulses that move from neuron to neuron. Dendrites are long fibers on neurons that carry messages into the nerve cell. Axons are long fibers on neurons that carry messages away from the nerve cell—and on to the next nerve cell. Between each neuron is a small gap, called a synapse. A special chemical carries the electrical impulse over this gap.

- Sensory neurons carry messages from the sense organs to the brain. Motor neurons carry messages from the brain to muscles. Relay neurons connect sensory and motor neurons.

- The brain has three main parts. The cerebrum controls muscle movement, thought, learning, memory, and the senses. The cerebellum coordinates muscles and helps with balance. The medulla controls the automatic functions of the body, such as breathing.

- Messages that are centered in the spinal cord rather than the brain are called reflexes. A reflex is an automatic and involuntary response to outside stimulation.

- Hormones are a different kind of body messenger. Hormones are released by glands. They travel in the bloodstream. They control such things as body growth and behavior.

Chapter Quiz

Write the answers to the following questions on a separate sheet of paper.

1. Describe the brain. What protects the brain?
2. Describe the spinal cord. What protects the spinal cord?
3. Explain the difference between axons and dendrites.
4. How do messages make it across synapses?
5. What does drinking alcohol do to the nervous system?
6. What would happen if there were no relay neurons in your nervous system?
7. What part of your brain keeps your heart beating?
8. How do reflexes protect you from harm?
9. How do hormones travel through the body?

The Brain in Three Parts

Here are some activities. Decide which part of the brain lets you do each one. On a separate sheet of paper, write "cerebrum," "cerebellum," or "medulla" next to the number for each activity.

1. Continue breathing.
2. Keep your balance walking across a log.
3. Learn to use a computer.
4. Digest food.
5. Remember your phone number.
6. Write a letter.
7. Think about someone you love.

Mad Scientist Challenge: Neuron Messengers

Suppose you step on a sharp rock. How will your foot get the message to lift off the rock before it gets hurt? Write a paragraph explaining the path of the message. Be sure to describe how the three kinds of neurons come into play.

Chapter 20

The Reproductive System

Louise Brown is the world's first test-tube baby. In what way is a test-tube baby different from other babies? How does any *baby develop from a single cell?*

Chapter Learning Objectives

- List the main organs of the male and female reproductive systems.
- Explain the menstrual cycle and its role in reproduction.
- Describe how human babies develop inside the mother.

Words to Know

embryo   the developing young after it has attached itself to the uterus

fetus   the offspring after fertilization of the egg but before birth; the last part of the development of the embryo

menopause   the time in a woman's life when she stops menstruating

menstruation   the monthly shedding of blood from a woman's uterus

ovaries   the female organs that make egg cells and hormones

oviducts   the tubes through which egg cells travel to the uterus

ovulation   the monthly release of an egg cell from an ovary

penis   the male organ that delivers sperm to the female

placenta   the structure through which food, oxygen, and wastes pass between the mother and the embryo

semen   the mixture of fluids in which sperm leaves the body

testes   the male organs that make sperm cells and hormones

urethra   the tube through which urine (and in males, also sperm) leaves the body

uterus   the female organ in which a fertilized egg develops into a baby

vagina   the canal that leads to the uterus

zygote   the cell that forms right after an egg cell has been fertilized

You may have heard about "test-tube" babies. This is how such a baby comes to be. First, an egg cell from a woman and sperm cells from a man are put in a test tube. With luck, the egg cell is fertilized by a sperm cell. Then doctors plant the fertilized egg cell in the woman's uterus. With even more luck, a baby will develop.

This way of producing a baby is only successful about one-fourth of the time. Scientists are still improving this process.

In this chapter you will learn how humans usually reproduce. You will also learn about the life cycle of humans—from two tiny cells to a full-grown person.

The Male Reproductive System

In sexual reproduction, an egg cell from the female joins with a sperm cell from the male. The male reproductive system has two functions. It must first produce sperm cells and then deliver them to the female reproductive system.

In males, sperm cells are made in organs called **testes**. The testes are in a sac of skin. To stay alive, sperm must be kept cooler than other parts of the body. The sac of skin keeps the sperm cool.

Sperm travels from the testes down thin tubes called *sperm ducts*. These ducts carry the sperm to the **urethra**. This is a tube in the **penis**. The penis delivers the sperm to the female reproductive system.

As the sperm moves down the sperm ducts and urethra, three glands add fluids to it. The mixture of sperm and the fluids is called **semen**.

Remember that humans are mammals. Mammals do not lay eggs. The offspring develop within the mother's body.

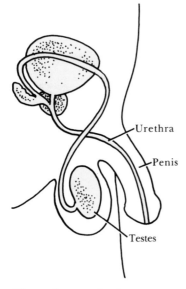

The male reproductive system

The reproductive organs in a boy's body begin maturing between the ages of 13 and 16. At this time, the testes make sex hormones. Remember that hormones are special substances that control certain body functions. Sex hormones in boys and men make thick face and body hair, a deep voice, and a muscular body.

The Female Reproductive System

Egg cells are made in the **ovaries** of females. The release of an egg is called **ovulation**. First, the egg moves into an oviduct, sometimes called the *fallopian tube*. Tiny hairs push the egg along its path. Then it moves down the oviduct to the **uterus**.

The uterus is a muscular, pear-shaped organ. It is hollow and has thick walls. This is where a baby develops if the egg cell is fertilized by a sperm cell.

If the egg is not fertilized, it passes out of the uterus. The egg moves down the **vagina**. This is the canal that leads from a woman's uterus to the outside of her body.

Like the male testes, ovaries also make hormones. This usually begins for girls between the ages of 10 and 14. Female sex hormones give women body hair, broad hips, and cause their breasts to develop. Another hormone helps the female body prepare the uterus for a baby.

The male sex hormone is called testosterone.

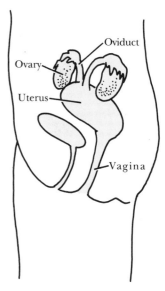

The female reproductive system

The female sex hormone is called estrogen.

Biology Practice

On a separate sheet of paper, write T for each sentence that is true and F for each sentence that is false.

1. Egg cells are made in the male testes.
2. Sperm cells are made in ovaries.
3. Tiny hairs in oviducts push the egg cells toward the uterus.
4. The organ in which a baby develops is called the urethra.
5. Sperm leaves the male body in a fluid called semen.

The Menstrual Cycle

In sexually mature women, an egg cell is released from the ovary about every 28 days. An egg cell lives one or two days. If in this time it is fertilized by a sperm cell, the woman becomes pregnant.

Each month the uterus prepares for the possibility of a baby. The walls of the uterus thicken and become swollen with blood. In this state, the uterus is prepared to nourish a developing baby.

Most of the time, however, the egg cell released each month is not fertilized. So the extra lining of the uterus breaks down. The lining is made of mucus, blood, and dead cells. This material leaves a woman's body through the vagina in a process called **menstruation.**

Menstruation usually lasts from 3 to 5 days. Shortly after menstruation, another egg cell matures in the ovary. Ovulation occurs about 14 days after menstruation. And then in another 14 days, menstruation occurs again. The cycle repeats itself about once a month.

Most girls begin menstruating some time between the ages of 10 and 14. Then, some time between the ages of 45 and 55, a woman's menstrual cycle stops. This end of menstruation is called **menopause.**

Women's menstrual cycles can vary a great deal. Some women menstruate as often as every 25 days. Others menstruate once every 30 days. The age at which women begin and end menstruation also varies a lot. Women have begun as early as 8 and as late as 20. Occasionally a woman will stop menstruating altogether before menopause is due. The cause of this is not always known. But sometimes the reason is emotional. A long-term fear or a serious worry can cause a woman to stop menstruating.

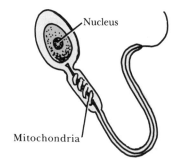

SPERM CELL

Nucleus

Mitochondria

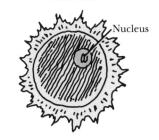

EGG CELL

Nucleus

Fertilization and Development

Males release millions of sperm at a time. Only one of these sperm has to join the egg cell for reproduction to occur. Once sperm is released into a female's vagina, sperm cells swim up the oviduct. Sperm cells swim by waving their tails. Fertilization usually happens in the oviduct. Once the sperm and egg cells have united, they are called a **zygote**. A membrane forms around the zygote. This keeps other sperm out.

Once in a while, a woman releases two eggs at once. If both eggs are fertilized, she will give birth to fraternal twins.

The zygote takes 4 or 5 days to travel to the uterus. As it travels, the zygote grows. By the time it reaches the uterus, it is made up of about 100 cells. This group of cells attaches itself to the uterus. It is now called an **embryo.**

A tissue called a **placenta** forms in the wall of the uterus. Food, oxygen, and wastes pass between the embryo and the mother through this structure.

However, the blood of the mother and the embryo never mix. The capillaries (tiny blood vessels) from both mother and embryo lie very close together in the placenta. Molecules of food and oxygen pass from the mother's blood into the embryo's blood. Molecules of wastes pass from the embryo's blood into the mother's blood.

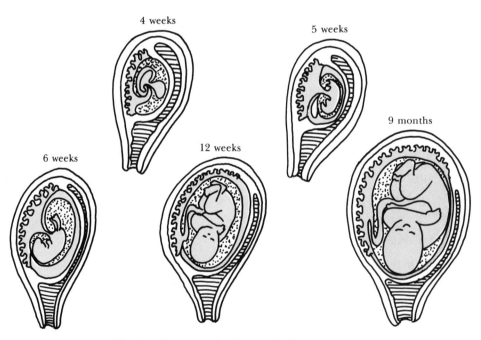

4 weeks

5 weeks

9 months

6 weeks

12 weeks

The development of a human baby

The embryo grows for about 9 months. In the later parts of its development, the embryo is called a **fetus**.

The fetus grows in a sac-like structure. Shortly before birth, this sac-like structure breaks. Strong muscle movements by the mother force the baby out of her body through the vagina. Shortly after the baby is born, the placenta is also pushed out of the mother's body. Soon the mother's breasts begin to secrete milk. This is a result of the impulses of hormones and nerves from the pregnancy.

On the Cutting Edge

"Prenatal" means before birth. Prenatal care means seeing a doctor regularly while pregnant. This can make a big difference in the health of a baby. There have been many great advances in caring for a pregnant woman and her fetus. One of the advances is called ultrasound, which uses soundwaves to see inside the mother's womb. With ultrasound, doctors can see how the baby is doing.

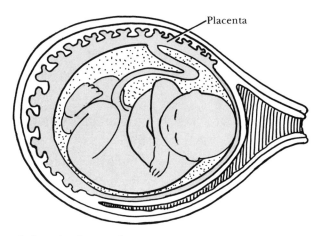

Placenta

A fetus in the womb

Chapter Review

Chapter Summary

- The main male reproductive organs are the testes, where sperm cells are made. Sperm cells travel from the testes through sperm ducts to the urethra. The urethra is a tube in the penis. Through the urethra, males release millions of sperm cells at a time.

- The main female reproductive organs are the ovaries, where egg cells are made. Egg cells are released one at a time, once a month. They travel through oviducts to the uterus. If the egg is not fertilized, it leaves a woman's body through the vagina.

- Sex hormones are produced in both the testes and ovaries. Male sex hormones give men deep voices, face and body hair, and muscular bodies. Female sex hormones give women body hair, broad hips, and cause their breasts to develop.

- Each month a woman's body prepares for pregnancy. The uterus swells with blood and mucus. If a fertilized egg does not enter the uterus, this lining of blood and mucus leaves the woman's body. This release of the uterus lining is called menstruation.

- Fertilization usually occurs in an oviduct. Once united, the egg and sperm cells are called a zygote. When the zygote attaches to the uterus, it becomes an embryo.

- The placenta is a structure in the uterus. There the capillaries of the embryo and the mother lie very close together. Food and oxygen molecules from the mother pass into the capillaries of the embryo. Wastes from the embryo pass into the capillaries of the mother.

Chapter Quiz

Write the answers to the following questions on a separate sheet of paper.

1. In what organs are sperm cells made?
2. In what organs are egg cells made?
3. What is the purpose of the sac of skin holding the testes?
4. Where are egg cells usually fertilized?
5. Why do blood and mucus leave a woman's body once a month? What is this process called?
6. Once an egg cell has been fertilized, what is it called?
7. When does a zygote become an embryo?

Reproductive Vocabulary

On a separate sheet of paper, write the word that best fits in each blank.

1. Males can release _____ of sperm cells at a time.
2. Females release _____ egg cell a month.
3. The mixture of sperm and other fluids is called _____.
4. Egg cells travel from the ovaries to the uterus by way of the _____.
5. A mother passes food and oxygen to her young through a tissue called the _____.

Mad Scientist Challenge: Reporting on the Fetus

The fetus does not simply sleep. Many fetuses are very active. The mother can feel her developing baby moving within her. Ask your mother how active you were before you were born. If you have any brothers or sisters, ask your mother how active they were compared to you. On a separate sheet of paper, write your answers.

Answer the following questions on a separate sheet of paper.

1. Which organ carries messages to the brain?

2. What is the central nervous system?

3. Why are vitamins important?

4. Name the five organs in the digestive system.

5. Name the four kinds of joints.

6. Describe the difference between voluntary and involuntary muscle.

7. Name the three kinds of neurons.

8. What is a reflex?

9. Name the three parts of the brain.

10. How is an egg fertilized in humans?

Living Together on Earth

Unit 6

Chapter 21

Ecology: The Web of Life

This spider is about ready to have dinner. Both the spider and the smaller insect are part of a food chain.

Chapter Learning Objectives

- Describe an ecosystem.
- Compare and contrast community, population, habitat, and niche.
- Describe how energy moves through ecosystems.
- Give an example of how organisms work together in partnerships.

Words to Know

community   all the living things in one ecosystem

consumers   organisms that cannot make their own food and must eat other organisms

decomposers   organisms that eat dead organisms and wastes

ecosystem   the series of relationships between a community of organisms and the environment

food web   many food chains that cross over one another

habitat   the place where an organism lives

mutualism   a symbiotic relationship in which both partners are helped

niche   the job function of an organism within an ecosystem

population   the group of one kind of organism living in an ecosystem

producers   organisms that make food by using energy from the sun

In the face of danger, an opossum rolls on its side. It kicks up its feet and lets its mouth hang open. The opossum makes its eyes go glassy. In short, it pretends to be dead until the danger goes away. A skunk deals with an enemy by letting out a terrible smell.

Creatures adapt to their environment over a long period of time. Adapting gives them a better chance to survive.

Other animals protect themselves by blending in with the environment. They do that to hide from their enemies. A walking stick is an insect that looks like a twig. A chameleon is a lizard that can change its skin color to blend in with the surroundings. The arctic fox has a gray or brown coat in the summer. It blends in with the rocks and plants. But in the winter it grows a white coat so it can blend in with snow.

All organisms live in a complex world. All organisms relate to many other organisms. They also relate to the many non-living parts of their environment. The relationship between living things and their environment is called *ecology.*

What Is an Ecosystem?

Your own town or city is an ecosystem of its own. What are some living things in your town or city? What are some non-living things?

Your surroundings make up your environment. There are both living and non-living things in your environment. All the living and non-living things together in an environment make an **ecosystem.** An ecosystem is the series of relationships between living things and their environment. For example, an ocean

A desert ecosystem

is an ecosystem. The ocean ecosystem includes fish, mammals, plants, algae, bacteria, soil on the ocean floor, rocks, salt water, and much more.

All together the living members of an ecosystem are called a **community**. In a desert ecosystem the community includes cactuses, jack rabbits, snakes, and lizards.

The group of *one kind* of organism in an ecosystem is called a **population**. In a forest ecosystem there is a population of deer. There may also be a population of birch trees, a population of mosses, and many other populations.

All of the populations in an ecosystem must contribute to the community. The community and the environment together create the ecosystem.

A Place and Job for Every Organism

Ecosystems, when left alone, are balanced. Every organism has a place to live, called a **habitat**. Soil is the habitat of earthworms. Wood is the habitat of termites.

Every organism also has a function within the ecosystem. This function or job is called a **niche**. For example, the function of green plants is to harness the energy of the sun. They use it to make food for the whole ecosystem. The function of spiders is to eat insects. This helps the ecosystem by keeping the insect population down. If there were no spiders, insects would eat all the plants.

Ecosystems change constantly. Think of a river ecosystem. Some kinds of birds come and go at certain times of year. Insects also leave and return. Fish get eaten or caught in the river. New fish hatch from eggs. River water evaporates. New water flows in from snow melt and smaller streams. Rain adds more water, too. Soil is washed downstream.

Like the systems of the human body, ecosystems are made of many parts working together. The parts are always adjusting to balance the ecosystem.

Every change in an ecosystem sets off other changes. This is how an ecosystem keeps in balance. Though some water leaves a river ecosystem, other water enters it. And while some fish are eaten or caught, other fish are born. An ecosystem is an area that is in balance.

On the Cutting Edge

Mistakes have taught biologists a lot about the balance of ecosystems. Some years ago, a community of plants, deer, coyotes, mountain lions, and wolves lived near the Grand Canyon. The deer ate the plants. The coyotes, mountain lions, and wolves ate the deer.

Some people felt sorry for the deer who were killed. So they began killing lots of coyotes, mountain lions, and wolves.

In a very short time, the whole ecosystem was thrown out of balance. The population of deer skyrocketed. But then there were not enough plants to feed all the new deer. Thousands of deer died of hunger. To keep them from eating all the plants, more deer had to be killed. In fact, the ecosystem was nicely balanced *before* people stepped in. The trouble started when people began killing the coyotes, mountain lions, and wolves.

The balance of ecosystems is not always easy to see. One small change can set off a lot of big changes. All of Earth is actually one big ecosystem. Biologists are working hard to understand the balance.

Energy Moves Around the Ecosystems

All ecosystems are powered by the sun. The sun is the ultimate source of energy for the living world. Plants absorb the energy of the sun directly. They trap the energy with their chlorophyll. Plants use the energy to make food by photosynthesis. Plants are **producers**. They make their own food.

Animals cannot make their own food. So they must eat plants or other animals to get their energy. Animals are **consumers**. They must get their food from other sources.

Together, plants and animals create an *energy cycle.* Plants use the sun's energy to make food. Animals consume the food for energy.

Decomposers complete the energy cycle. Decomposers are mostly bacteria. They eat dead organisms and the waste products of animals. Decomposers return the nutrients of these organisms to the soil. The plants use the recycled nutrients to grow more food and start the cycle again.

The entire ecosystem is built around the energy cycle. If the energy cycle is interrupted, the ecosystem will fail.

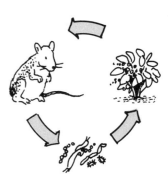

Energy cycle

Amazing Biology

Plants trap only one percent of the sun energy that reaches Earth. This is a tiny bit when you think of all the energy produced by the sun. But this tiny bit of energy gives life to all organisms.

Food Webs

You've read about food chains. Most organisms belong to more than one food chain. Usually food chains in an ecosystem cross over one another. Animals in one food chain often eat animals in other food chains. This is called a **food web**.

Here's an example of a food web. Snakes eat things like mice, insects, rabbits, and frogs. The snake is food for hawks, owls, bobcats, and other animals. Besides the snake, a hawk might eat rabbits, birds, or mice.

Most animals that eat other animals only kill the sick, weak, and aged in a population. How does this practice help keep an ecosystem in balance?

A food web

Partnerships Between Organisms

Sometimes organisms work very closely together as partners. You have read about parasites. A *parasitic relationship* is a partnership in which one of the organisms is harmed and one helped. Fleas, for example, are parasites on dogs and cats.

You have also read about symbiosis, or a *symbiotic relationship*. In this case, at least one of the partners is helped by the partnership. The other partner is at least not harmed. **Mutualism** is a symbiotic relationship that benefits both partners.

For example, a honeybee gathers nectar from a plant's flower. This gives food to the bee. And the bee helps pollinate the flower.

Lichen is another example of mutualism. Lichen is actually two kinds of organisms, fungi and algae, living together. The algae carry out photosynthesis to make food which also feeds the fungi. In turn, the fungi supply water and minerals for the algae.

You are in partnership with bacteria. These bacteria live inside your large intestine. They help to remove water from waste food that hasn't been digested. These bacteria also help to produce vitamin K. In return, you give the bacteria a place to live and food to eat.

There are many partnerships in an ecosystem. Many organisms work together to survive.

You are the ecosystem of the bacteria. The bacteria work to keep the ecosystem (you) in balance and working properly.

Chapter Review

Chapter Summary

- All the living and non-living things together in an environment make an ecosystem. The group of living things in an ecosystem is called a community. The group of one kind of organism is called a population. The place where an organism lives is called its habitat. And the job an organism has within the community is called its niche.

- All ecosystems are powered by the sun. The energy moves through food chains. Most organisms are a part of several food chains, called a food web. Plants are called producers because they make the food for an ecosystem. Animals, fungi, and some bacteria are consumers.

- Decomposers are at the bottom of food chains. They eat dead organisms and wastes. They are very important to ecosystems because they return nutrients to the soil. When plants use these nutrients, the energy cycle begins again.

- Many organisms work in partnerships with others. In a parasitic relationship, one partner is helped and one is harmed. In a symbiotic relationship, at least one of the partners is helped. And the other partner is at least not harmed. Mutualism is a symbiotic relationship in which both partners are helped.

Chapter Quiz

Write the answers to the following questions on a separate sheet of paper.

1. What is an ecosystem?
2. Name five living and five non-living things in your classroom environment.
3. Name five different kinds of organisms found in a city community.
4. What is the human population in your biology class?
5. Describe the habitat of a frog.
6. Describe the habitat of a tree in a park.
7 Are pine trees producers, consumers, or decomposers?
8. Are people producers, consumers, or decomposers?
9. Think of a pond ecosystem. Name three changes that might happen regularly.
10. Give one example of mutualism.

Food Chains

On a separate sheet of paper, draw a food chain. Show and label one producer, one consumer, and one decomposer.

Mad Scientist Challenge: Rain Forests

The rain forests in South America have their own balanced ecosystem. Many of these rain forests are now being cut down. The land is being used for cattle. Make a list of all the ways you can think of that the rain forest ecosystem is being changed. You may want to use the encyclopedia. Look up the kinds of plants and animals found in rain forests. Think how the loss of trees will change their lives.

Chapter 22

The Cycles of Life

Water vapor from the Chicago River rises into the air on a cold winter day. What do you think will happen to the water vapor? Where does the water in the river come from?

Chapter Learning Objectives

- Explain the water cycle.
- Explain the importance of the oxygen and carbon-dioxide cycle.
- Describe how bacteria change nitrogen into nitrates for other organisms.

Words to Know

condense to change from a gas into a liquid

evaporate to change from a liquid to a gas

greenhouse effect what happens when too much carbon dioxide on Earth traps the sun's heat

nitrates a form of nitrogen that can be used by cells for making proteins

nitrogen-fixing changing nitrogen gas into a usable form for life

pollution any foreign substance harmful to the ecosystem

Think about the last time you had a glass of water. Now think about where that water had been before you drank it. It's possible that it could have been part of a swamp where alligators swam. It could have fallen as rain in Italy. Or it could have been given off by plants in Africa as a waste product of respiration.

The point is that all water is recycled. That means it is used over and over again. The same is true for oxygen, carbon dioxide, and nitrogen. These important life substances must be shared—used and reused—by all life on Earth.

In this chapter you will learn how water, oxygen, carbon dioxide, and nitrogen are recycled.

The Water Cycle

Water is in movement all the time. Think of the ocean. As the sun shines down on it and the surface water warms up enough, it **evaporates**. That means it turns into a gas, called water vapor. The water vapor rises off the ocean surface. It goes up into the sky.

After a while the water vapor cools down. When water vapor cools, it **condenses**. That means the gas turns back into a liquid. The water vapor condenses into tiny droplets which make clouds. In the clouds, the tiny droplets combine into heavier and heavier drops of water. When the drops are heavy enough, it rains. If the temperature is very cold, water can turn to snow or sleet as it falls to Earth.

Some of the rain, snow, or sleet sinks into the soil. Plants use the water. Later, the plants will give off some of the water as water vapor.

Some of the rain, snow, or sleet runs off the ground and into lakes and rivers. Small rivers run into larger rivers. Eventually larger rivers dump their water into the sea. From there the cycle starts all over again.

Think about the water cycle. Why do you think it's important to keep lake, river, and sea water clean?

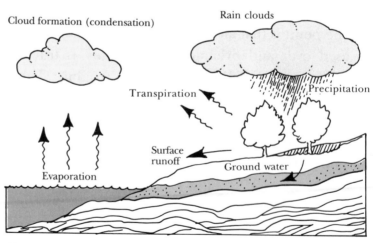

The water cycle

The Oxygen and Carbon-Dioxide Cycle

As you know, plants give off oxygen as a waste product of photosynthesis. You—and most other animals—breathe in the oxygen that plants give off. When you use this oxygen for respiration, you get energy from food and oxygen.

You breathe out water vapor and carbon dioxide as wastes. That same carbon dioxide is used by plants again for photosynthesis. The gas exchange between photosynthesis and respiration is at the heart of the cycle.

Even underwater ecosystems have an oxygen cycle. Fish take oxygen from the water through their gills. They exhale carbon dioxide into the water. The algae and marine plants use the carbon dioxide in photosynthesis. The algae and marine plants put oxygen back into the water. This way they maintain the underwater ecosystem.

The ecosystem must adjust constantly to maintain the vital life cycles.

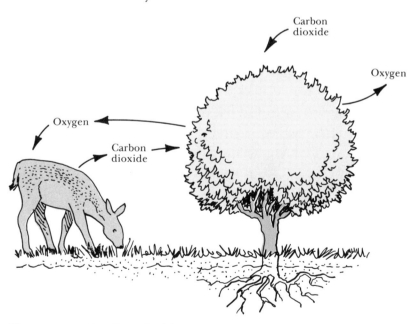

The oxygen and carbon-dioxide cycle

Biology Practice

On a separate sheet of paper, write the word that best goes in each blank.

1. When the sun shines down on the ocean, water _____ off the surface.
2. Plants and animals give off water _____ as a waste product of respiration.
3. Plants give off _____ as a waste product of photosynthesis.
4. The carbon dioxide that animals breathe out is used by plants for _____ .

Biology Alert

Nothing in the atmosphere simply vanishes. Everything is exchanged and recycled. That is why **pollution** is so dangerous. It never truly goes away. Our careless ways come back to haunt us.

Right now, the United States and Canada are very concerned about acid rain. Acid rain is caused by industrial pollution. How is it formed? When ash and smoke rise from factories, they join with the water vapor in clouds. Then, when the vapor cools, the ash and smoke fall back to Earth with the rain. Acid rain is poisonous. Many people fear that the food chain and water cycle may carry the poisons back to us.

On the Cutting Edge

More and more of Earth's forests are being cut down. The great rain forests in South America are quickly disappearing. The land is being used for cattle grazing and other things.

As a result, there are fewer plants using carbon-dioxide for photosynthesis. So too much carbon-dioxide is building up in the air surrounding the Earth.

This blanket of carbon dioxide traps heat on Earth. Scientists call this the **"greenhouse effect."** It may be causing the Earth to become warmer and warmer. If the process is not stopped, people on Earth may face long, dry hot spells in the future. This weather change may make it very difficult to grow food.

Everyone agrees that we should stop polluting the air. And most people believe we must also stop cutting down forest.

South American rain forests are being cut down.

The Nitrogen Cycle

All living things need nitrogen. Nitrogen is one of the most important nutrients that help to form cell proteins.

Getting nitrogen shouldn't be a problem. Almost 78 percent of the air is nitrogen. But plants and animals are not able to use nitrogen directly from the air. Nitrogen cannot be processed by respiration. So the nitrogen must be changed into a form that plants and animals can eat. Nitrogen must be processed by the digestive system. To do this, nitrogen must be changed into another form called **nitrates**. A special kind of bacteria changes nitrogen from the air into nitrates. The process of change is called **nitrogen-fixing**.

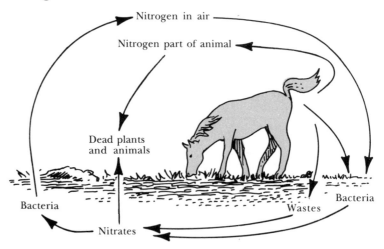

The nitrogen cycle

After bacteria take the nitrogen from the air, they change it into nitrates. These nitrates go into the soil. Plants soak up the nitrates with water in their roots. The nitrates become a part of the plants. When animals eat the plants, they get the nitrates, too.

When plants and animals die, other kinds of bacteria break down the organisms. The nitrates are returned to the soil. From there they are recycled back into plants.

Then still other kinds of bacteria change the nitrates in the soil back into nitrogen gas. This gas goes back into the air. So the cycle continues.

Decomposers break dead animals and wastes down into nitrates. So the energy cycle and the nitrogen cycle are closely related.

The Balancing Act

All the life cycles are taking place at once. That means the ecosystems must have enough water, oxygen, carbon dioxide, and nitrogen at all times. To stay in balance, the cycles must not be interrupted.

However, people often try to change ecosystems to solve short-term problems. We use chemical additives to make soil more fertile. We use pesticides to kill insects that harm farm crops. We cut down forests for lumber. We get rid of wastes by throwing them into the water. These short-term solutions sometimes cause bigger, long-term problems.

People are just beginning to understand the balance of Earth's ecosystems. We are dependent on all other parts of the ecosystem. If we destroy one part of it, we are only hurting ourselves.

On the Cutting Edge

In September 1991, four women and four men were sealed inside a giant glass and steel structure in the middle of the Arizona desert. They were planning to live there for two years.

The structure is called Biosphere 2. The crew members are part of an experiment to see if it is possible to create a self-contained environment. Biosphere 2 is larger than two football fields. It has five different ecosystems, including a tiny 25-foot deep ocean, a savanna, a desert, a rain forest, and a marsh. There are 3,800 species of plants and animals living in Biosphere 2. The air, water, and wastes are all recycled in this closed environment. The crew grow their own crops and raise their own livestock. They can communicate with the outside world by telephone and fax machine.

In early 1993, Biosphere 2 did not have enough oxygen. Crew members began to get weak. So oxygen from the outside was pumped into the structure. Biosphere 2 was no longer self-supporting. However, the scientists running the experiment say they were not "cheating." This was exactly the kind of problem they wanted to study. Now they want to find out *why* the plants in Biosphere 2 didn't produce enough oxygen.

Some people consider Biosphere 2 a practice space colony. If people can create a self-sustaining environment on Earth, then we will be able to develop communities in space.

Biosphere 2 in the Arizona desert.

Biology Alert

Americans throw out an average of 3.5 pounds of trash daily. All together, this is about 160 million tons a year. Add in other garbage like mining wastes and sludge, and the number of tons a year goes up to 11 billion.

We are quickly running out of places to put garbage and other wastes. In 1990, about 80 percent of our garbage was buried in landfills. The Environmental Protection Agency believes that more than a third of our country's landfills are full. People fight having new dumps put in their communities. So garbage is being hauled greater distances and costing people more.

Creating less garbage is the only solution to this problem. People must buy reusable products rather than disposable ones. Paper and other products such as glass, scrap metal, scrap wood, and plastic can be recycled.

Chapter Review

Chapter Summary

- All water on Earth is recycled. Water evaporates off oceans, rivers, lakes, and soil. The water vapor goes up into the air. There it condenses into tiny droplets of water and forms clouds. When the droplets combine into heavier drops, they fall to Earth as rain, snow, or sleet. Some of the water sinks into soil. It is used by plants. Some of the water runs into rivers and lakes. Rivers carry the water to the sea.

- Oxygen and carbon dioxide are recycled by plants and animals. Plants give off oxygen as a waste of photosynthesis. Animals use the oxygen in respiration. They give off carbon dioxide as a waste. Plants use this carbon dioxide in photosynthesis. This exchange is at the center of the cycles of life.

- All living things need nitrogen for making proteins. The air is 78 percent nitrogen. But animals can't get nitrogen by respiration. Bacteria change this nitrogen gas into nitrates in the soil. This process is called nitrogen-fixing. Plants use the nitrates in the soil. Animals get the nitrates from eating the plants. When plants and animals die, other bacteria get the nitrates and put them back into the soil. Still other bacteria change the nitrates back into nitrogen gas. This nitrogen gas goes back into the air.

Chapter Quiz

Write the answers to the following questions on a separate sheet of paper.

1. How does the water you drink get to you? Name at least three steps.
2. How does water get up into the air?
3. Where does the oxygen on the Earth come from?
4. What waste product of respiration do plants use in photosynthesis?
5. What could happen if the "greenhouse effect" got worse?
6. Why must all living things have nitrogen?
7. What form must nitrogen take before plants and animals can use it?
8. How do bacteria help plants to get nitrates?
9. How do animals get nitrates?

Solving Environmental Problems

On a separate sheet of paper, write a sentence describing what should be done about the following environmental problems:

1. Acid Rain
2. The "Greenhouse Effect"
3. Pesticides

Mad Scientist Challenge: Class Discussion

You have studied three cycles: the water cycle, the oxygen and carbon-dioxide cycle, and the nitrogen cycle. All these substances must be used over and over again by living things on Earth.

Think about the effects of air and water pollution. What does this pollution have to do with the three cycles you have studied? What do you think should be done about pollution?

Chapter 23

Behavior of Living Things

Birds build nests to protect their eggs. How does the bird know how to build a nest? How does it know what materials to use?

Chapter Learning Objectives
- Describe the difference between instincts and learned behavior.
- Give two examples of how animals live and work together in groups or families.
- Define hibernation and migration.
- Describe two ways that animals communicate.

Words to Know

behavior   the way an organism responds to the environment; all the actions of an organism

biological clock   a timing process in animals, perhaps controlled by hormones, that lets them know when to eat, sleep, mate, hibernate, and migrate

conditioning   the way learned behavior is taught

hibernation   a long rest during which an animal's heartbeat and breathing rate slow down; many animals *hibernate* during the winter

instinct   behavior that is known from birth

pheromones   the chemical signals some animals use to affect or attract other animals of the same species

Some people play soothing music for their plants. They believe that music may help plants grow. Suppose biologists were to test this idea in the lab. They would be studying the way living things act or behave.

In this chapter you will learn about the behavior of living things. **Behavior** is the way an organism responds to the environment. Simple organisms have simple responses. The more complex the organism, the more complex the behavior. Most of this chapter will be about animal behavior.

Instincts and Learned Behavior

A baby mammal knows to drink its mother's milk. No one ever teaches the baby this trick. Behavior that is known from birth is called an **instinct**. Instincts are inherited.

Biologists define six areas of instinct. These are nutrition, aggression, reproduction, sleep, grooming, and grouping. The nutrition instinct means that the animals know what to eat. Aggression means they know who their enemies are. Reproduction means the animals know how to mate and bear their young. Grooming means they know how to clean themselves. And grouping means animals know how to behave with their own kind.

Knowing how to make honey is an instinct in bees. Nest-building is an instinct in birds. Dam-building is an instinct in beavers. Birds and beavers know how to build without anyone ever teaching them. Other animals can swim by instinct.

Instincts are one way an organism adapts to its environment over many generations. Eventually, the instincts become part of the organism's genetic code.

A beaver builds a dam by instinct.

Instinctive behavior accounts for many of the ways animals behave. But many animals can learn more than what they know by instinct. For example, a bird can learn from one of its parents to build a *better* nest. It can learn where to find good materials. It can learn what kinds of trees are best for nesting.

Birds also fly by instinct. But they may need encouragement. A parent bird will nudge the baby bird. The parent may even fly under or near the baby until it feels safe flying. A sea otter may also need encouragement before it begins to swim.

Many of the ways animals behave are learned. *Learned behavior* comes from training or **conditioning**. A sea otter learns to use a stone to crack open mussel shells. It may learn this by watching another otter. Or it may learn it by accident. One day it might drop a mussel on a rock and see it crack. Either way, the behavior of cracking open mussels with rocks is learned behavior.

Problem-solving is a high level of learning. Are humans the only animals that can solve problems? Primates, such as chimpanzees, and sea mammals, such as dolphins, are some of the smartest animals. Biologists try to find out what kinds of problems these animals can solve. Dolphins can find their way through an underwater obstacle course. Chimpanzees can use sticks as tools and weapons. They will stack boxes to climb up and reach bananas.

A dog or cat might figure out how to open a door or window by itself. This is an example of problem-solving.

Mating and Families

How do animals behave in groups? Some animals prefer to live by themselves. Others live or work in families or groups.

Mammals care for their young until they can care for themselves. Mother mammals are almost always involved in raising their young. This is because they must feed the young with their own milk. Sometimes male mammals help in raising their young. Father wolves stay with the mother and pups. The entire pack cares for all the pups. Wolves, and also foxes, seem to mate for life.

On the other hand, the care of lion cubs is handled only by females. All females in a pride (group) of lions help care for all the cubs. Mouse-eared bats actually set up nurseries for babies and the females. Male bats are not allowed in the nurseries.

Female birds do not feed their young with their own milk. So males can take on the job of raising the young as well as females. Father birds often help the mother in raising the family. Some birds, such as geese, swans, and some eagles, mate for life.

Amazing Biology

The male rhea, a bird of South America, builds the nest all by himself. Then he gathers eggs from several females. He may get as many as 30 eggs to put in his nest. Then he sits on the eggs until they hatch. The male rhea also protects the young birds until they can go out on their own.

Working in Groups

Many animals work together to get food and protect themselves. Musk oxen, for example, live in small herds in the Arctic. Wolves often attack the musk oxen. To protect their young, the adult oxen make a wall in front of the calves. One male steps forward to warn off the wolves. If he is killed, another ox moves forward. One by one, the oxen move forward to protect the herd until the wolves leave.

Wolves work together, too. They hunt in groups. This teamwork gives them a better chance of making a kill.

Honeybees have the most amazing organization of work. There are three kinds of honeybees in a hive. Usually there is just one *queen bee.* Her job is to lay eggs so the hive will have offspring. *Drones* are male honeybees. Their job is to produce sperm to fertilize the queen's eggs. *Worker bees* do many jobs in their lives. First, they are "nurse bees." They feed and care for young bees. Later, they are "house bees." They clean, store honey, produce wax, and guard the hive. Adult workers become "field bees." They collect nectar from plants.

A beehive

Biology Practice

Write the answers to the following questions on a separate sheet of paper.

1. Give two examples of instinctive behavior.
2. Give two examples of learned behavior.
3. A chimpanzee will strip the leaves off a plant and use the stem to catch ants. What is this an example of?
4. Why do some animals live in groups? Give an example of group behavior.

Hibernation

Some animals go into **hibernation** for several months of the year. Hibernation is more than a deep sleep. The body temperature of hibernating animals goes down. They take fewer breaths a minute and their heartbeat slows down, too. For example, a hibernating marmot's heart may beat only 23 times in an hour.

Before hibernating, mammals eat lots of high-energy foods. They build a thick layer of fat around their bodies. They live off this fat during hibernation. Potassium builds up in their blood, too. The potassium helps to keep body cells from freezing, much like an *antifreeze*.

Mammals that hibernate include chipmunks, squirrels, hamsters, marmots, bats, and bears. But mammals are not the only animals that hibernate. So do certain birds, such as nighthawks and swifts. And cold-blooded animals such as frogs, toads, lizards, snakes, and turtles also hibernate. When cold weather causes the body temperature of amphibians or reptiles to drop, the animals enter hibernation. They can be awakened from hibernation when the environment warms up enough to heat their bodies.

A bear hibernates during the winter.

Most plants do not grow much or at all during the winter months. In the spring, with rain and sunshine, they grow a lot. Do you think plants go through a kind of hibernation of their own?

Migration

Animals migrate for different reasons. Whales migrate to the south so they can give birth to their young in warm waters. Other animals migrate to warmer areas in the winter because they cannot survive the cold. Mule deer spend summers in high elevations and winters in lower elevations. They do this because that's where the best food is at these times of the year.

At the end of each summer, Caribbean lobsters crawl across the ocean floor in long lines. The lobsters are headed for the warmer waters of the Bahamas. When salmon are ready to lay eggs, they migrate to the place

Salmon swimming upstream

where they were born. Salmon are born in rivers. So migrating salmon must leave the ocean and swim against the river current to the places of their birth.

Animals prepare for migration by storing extra fat. This gives their bodies extra energy.

Amazing Biology

Lemmings are mouse-like rodents found in the northern parts of the world. Lemmings may carry out the strangest of all migrations. Every three or four years, huge groups of lemmings come down from the mountains of Norway. They try to swim across rivers and even the sea. Many of them drown. Why do they set out on these death marches?

What happens is that in certain years food is very plentiful. In those years, the lemmings reproduce very, very quickly. The lemming population becomes huge. Then there are too many lemmings for the food supply. So the lemmings migrate to look for food and a new place to live.

Biological Clocks

Morning glories, a kind of flower, close up every afternoon. Many animals get sleepy every night. Others wake up at night. How do plants and animals know when to do things?

It seems that living things have what scientists call **biological clocks**. These biological clocks let animals know when to sleep, eat, mate, migrate, and hibernate.

Birds use their biological clock to help navigate. Their biological clock tells them how long they've flown.

Biology Alert

Have you ever flown across the country in an airplane? If you have, you crossed a few time zones. When it is 10:00 p.m. in New York, it is only 7:00 p.m. in San Francisco. It sometimes takes a few days to adjust to the new time schedule. This is called "jet lag." Your biological clock gets confused.

Scientists believe that daylight helps the biological clock work. For example, in the fall there are fewer hours of daylight. This sets off something, perhaps hormones, in the bodies of animals that hibernate. They begin to build up fat to prepare for hibernation. The number of hours of daylight may also trigger animals to prepare for migration.

Avoiding Danger

Animals have many ways of avoiding danger. Some, like cats, can run fast. The armadillo can't run fast. But it has a hard covering of plates to protect it. Porcupines have sharp, pointed needles that can kill other animals.

Some animals have colorings that protect them. Green frogs blend in with the plants around lakes and rivers. The snowshoe rabbit is reddish brown in the summer. This helps it to blend in with the summer environment. Its coat changes to white in the winter to blend in with the snow.

Animal Communication

Animals have many different ways of communicating with one another. They make sounds, give off scents, do dances, touch each other, give off light signals, and change colors.

Birds use their songs to say who they are. The songs also attract mates, warn of danger, and tell other birds of their territory. Male peacocks spread their beautiful tails to get a female's attention.

Fireflies flash light signals to one another. The pattern and color of the flashes tell what kind of firefly is signalling. A male firefly may flash a signal when he is ready to mate. A female flashes a signal back. She signals where she is and what kind of firefly she is.

Ants use chemicals to communicate. These chemical signals are called **pheromones**. The ants go out to find food. When an ant finds some, it brings it back to the nest. And as it comes back, it leaves a trail of pheromones. The other ants follow the scent of the pheromones back to the food. As they return to the nest, they also leave scent trails. The scent gets

Many other animals besides ants use pheromones. Some animals use pheromones to mark their territory or attract mates.

A male peacock spreads it feathers to attract a female.

stronger. More and more ants follow the trail until the food supply is gone.

Honeybees carry out very complex dances to describe where to find food. The dances are like detailed maps.

Bats and dolphins both get information by using sound waves. The sound waves they send out bounce off objects and return. Dolphins and bats can read a lot from these returning sound waves. They know the size of the object that the waves bounced off. They also know where the object is. This is why bats are able to fly in the dark.

People in Biology: Eloy Rodriguez

Eloy Rodriguez, a biology professor, studies the leaves that chimpanzees eat.

While studying chimps in the wild, Rodriguez watched a sick chimp as she broke off a shoot from a plant and sucked out the juice. By the next day, the chimp was feeling good again. After studying the chemistry of the plant, Rodriguez found that it contained a medicine. He and other scientists have identified at least 15 plant species that the chimps use to cure ailments.

The chimps may lead people to some useful medicines. Rodriguez noticed that some mornings the chimps walked 20 minutes to a particular plant. They would gulp the leaves whole and then make faces at how bad-tasting the plant was. Rodriguez found that the plant has a red oil in it that kills parasites, fungi, and viruses. Scientists have found that this plant kills cancer cells.

Chapter Review

Chapter Summary

- Behavior is the way living things respond to their environment. Some behaviors are known by animals from birth. These behaviors are called instincts. Other behaviors must be learned. The highest form of learning is problem-solving.

- There is great variety in the family life of animals. Most female mammals care for their young. Some male mammals help. Male birds often help in caring for the young.

- Many kinds of animals work together in packs or herds to get food or protect themselves. Honeybees have very organized work roles.

- Some animals hibernate during times when food is hard to find. They usually eat a lot of high-energy foods before going into hibernation. They live off the fat stored on their bodies. Other animals migrate to warmer places or better feeding grounds.

- Plants and animals have biological clocks to let them know when to do certain things. Scientists think that the number of daylight hours sets off hormones. These hormones direct the biological clocks. This is how animals know when to hibernate and migrate.

- Animals have different ways to protect themselves. Some can move quickly. Others have protective coverings. Still others have coats that blend in with the environment.

- Scientists study the many ways that animals communicate with one another. Many animals communicate by sound, scent, or touch. Some animals use chemical signals, called pheromones.

Chapter Quiz

Write the answers to the following questions on a separate sheet of paper.

1. What is an instinct? Give two examples of instinctive behavior.

2. What is conditioning? Give two examples of learned behavior.

3. Why are mammal mothers almost always involved in raising young?

4. Give two reasons why animals might work together in groups.

5. Describe what goes on in an animal's body during hibernation.

6. How does a bird's body prepare for migration?

7. Describe three different ways that animals protect themselves from danger.

8. What kinds of things are birds communicating with their songs?

9. How do ants let others know where to find food?

What Kind of Behavior?

Here is a list of behaviors. On a separate sheet of paper, write "instinctive" or "learned" for each one.

1. a mammal drinking its mother's milk

2. a beaver building a dam

3. a runner practicing her start

Mad Scientist Challenge: Be a Psychologist

Psychologists study *human* behavior. Think a little bit about human behavior. Then answer the following questions on a separate sheet of paper.

1. How do people behave when they are frightened?

2. How do people behave when they are hungry?

3. How do people behave when they are very happy?

Chapter 24

Resources for Life

In many places today people are cutting down the forests. Do you think this is a good idea? What would happen to the Earth if there were no forests left?

Chapter Learning Objectives

- Name four important natural resources.
- List two ways that natural resources can be conserved.
- Describe three ways to stop pollution.

Words to Know

conservation   the wise use and protection of natural resources

endangered species   organisms in danger of becoming extinct

erosion   the wearing away of topsoil

extinct   no longer existing

natural resources   the things on Earth that people need to live

non-renewable resources   resources that are in limited supply

renewable resources   resources that can be resupplied

reservoirs   lakes that people build to save water

topsoil   the upper layer of rich, dark soil in which plants grow

There are well over 5,000,000,000 (five billion) people on Earth today. Scientists say that the human population will double in just a few more years. Can Earth support this many people? Are there enough of the things people need to live?

In this chapter you will learn about the supplies of **natural resources** on Earth. The natural resources that people need to live include minerals, water, air, soil, plants, and other animals.

Natural Resources and Conservation

Conservation is the wise use and protection of natural resources. Some of these resources are **renewable resources**. This means that people can add to the supply. For example, trees are a renewable resource. When trees are cut down, more trees can be planted. But even renewable resources must be used with care. It takes time to replace what we use. New trees can be grown. But they can take more than fifty years to reach full size.

Minerals, such as iron, copper, and sulfur, are **non-renewable resources**. Once all these minerals are taken from the Earth, they are gone. People cannot make any more. But we can recycle the metals we do use.

What other renewable resources can you think of? How can they be renewed?

On the Cutting Edge

How would you like to be a miner living and working on an asteroid? An asteroid is a small planet-like object between the orbits of Mars and Jupiter. Scientists say there are mineral deposits on asteroids, the moon, and on other planets. One day, if we run out of minerals on Earth, people may start mining asteroids. A colony of people might live in space to be close to their work. Or it's possible that robot miners could gather minerals for us.

Water

Chicago gets its water from Lake Michigan. Los Angeles gets its water from the Colorado River. Many cities store their water in big **reservoirs**. These are human-made lakes built to hold water for a community.

How much water do you use each day? Consider all your uses of water: bathing, drinking, watering gardens and lawns, washing clothes and dishes, flushing toilets. But that is only a small part of your water use. Farms and factories use huge amounts of water. And you use the food and products made by farms and factories. So if you add it all up, you probably use many hundreds of gallons a day!

You have already studied the water cycle. You know that the same water must be used over and over. Water pollution is a problem for every living thing that uses water.

Where does your city store its water? Does it have a reservoir?

A reservoir and water purifying plant

Pollution is anything harmful that enters the environment. Water pollution can be caused by many things. Factories sometimes dump wastes in rivers and lakes. Human wastes, called *sewage,* are sometimes dumped in rivers and lakes, as well. Chemical fertilizers from farms also pollute the water.

Most cities have laws about dumping wastes into lakes and rivers. Most cities also have sewage treatment plants. These plants treat raw sewage with chemicals. That makes the sewage safe to return to the water supply. But chemical fertilizers are harder to keep out of the water supply. These fertilizers are put on soil. They wash away with the rains or sink into the underground water supply. Keeping them out of the water system is very important.

Biology Alert

The Cuyahoga River in Cleveland, Ohio was so polluted in 1969 that it caught fire! Since then it has been cleaned up. Today, Clevelanders enjoy their clean riverfront.

Air

How much air do you use every day? That is a hard question to answer. But your respiratory system needs lots of clean air to keep you alive. Like water, air is a non-renewable resource. The air around the Earth is all the air we have.

Factories and cars are the biggest polluters of the air. When fossil fuels are burned, they release solid particles, soot, carbon dioxide, and other poisonous gases into the air.

Some of the poisonous gases mix with water vapor in the air to make a strong acid. This acid can hurt the eyes and lungs of people and other animals. The acids also can harm the growth of certain food crops and other plants.

Rain washes these acids out of the air. These rains are called "acid rains." The poisons then become a part of the water cycle.

People must take steps to stop air pollution. For acid rain to stop, sulfur must be taken out of fossil fuels. To stop other kinds of pollution, the solid particles from burned fossil fuels must be kept out of the air. This can be done in two ways. One, factory smokestacks can have filters. The filters stop small particles from going into the air. And two, fuels can be burned more completely. The more a fuel is burned, the less material is left to go into the air.

Using much less fossil fuel can also help to stop air pollution. It helps if people take buses and subways instead of cars. And it helps to ride to work in groups so that fewer cars are used.

Fossil fuels are the remains of plants and animals from millions of years ago. Coal, oil, and natural gas are all fossil fuels. They are burned for energy.

Remember that everything in the ecosystem is related. The pollution of one part of the cycle of life will eventually affect all of it.

Biology Alert

Fluorocarbons are another type of air pollutant. Fluorocarbons are used in spray cans and plastics. They are released into the atmosphere as a gas. Fluorocarbons destroy the ozone in the *ozone layer*. The ozone layer is a thin layer of oxygen in the Earth's atmosphere. It blocks dangerous radiation from the sun. The use of fluorocarbons has badly damaged the ozone layer. Many countries are getting together to ban the use of fluorocarbons.

Biology Practice

Below is a list of natural resources. Think about how each resource can be used wisely by people. On a separate sheet of paper, write down one thing people can do to conserve each resource.

1. trees   2. water   3. minerals   4. air

Soil

In Chapter 8, you learned that soil is made up of bits of rock and plants and animals. The sand, silt, and clay particles are all minerals. They provide nutrients to the green plants. The humus, the organic part of the soil, provides more nutrients. The humus is very important. It must be replenished with the remains of dead plants and animals.

Only topsoil has humus in it. **Topsoil** is the rich, top layer of soil in which all plants grow. *Subsoil* is the soil below topsoil. Subsoil is made of only rock particles. *Bedrock*, below the subsoil, is solid rock.

Topsoil is a non-renewable resource. It takes hundreds of years just to form one inch of topsoil. Many forces in the environment cause soil to form. The sun heats rock. At night the rock cools and cracks. In winter, ice hardens in the cracks and breaks up the rock even more. Rain also wears down rock over hundreds of years. And when plant roots grow in the cracks, they also help break up the rock.

People need topsoil in order to grow food. However, conserving topsoil is not easy. Important minerals in soil get used up by growing plants over and over in the same soil. Farmers can add fertilizers to add nutrients back to the soil. They can also *rotate crops*. That means growing different kinds of crops in different fields from year to year. They can also let some fields rest for a year or two.

Fertilizers help preserve the topsoil. But chemical fertilizers can threaten the water supply. They must be used very carefully or they will poison the ground.

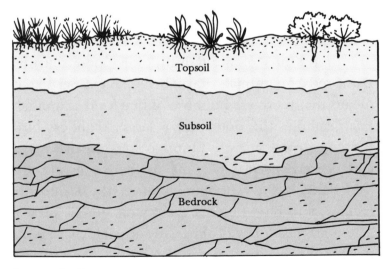

Layers of soil

Erosion is a serious problem for farmers. This is the wearing away of topsoil. Water and wind are the biggest causes of erosion.

Planting ground covers in between crops can help to prevent erosion. For example, corn is a tall crop. The soil under the corn is open to wind and rain. It can easily blow or wash away. If a farmer plants a low-growing plant between the rows of corn, the plants will hold the soil in place.

Farmers can also grow *windbreaks*. These are rows of trees that block the wind. They protect fields from erosion by wind.

Forests and Wildlife

Paper is a wood product. Many homes are built of lumber made from trees. However, people like to use the forests for camping and hiking, too. And Earth's forests are also home to many plants and animals, so people must use forest resources wisely.

Wild plants and animals, called *wildlife*, are another natural resource. Wildlife can be found in deserts, grasslands, rivers, lakes, fields, and forests.

As the human population has grown, the number of other kinds of animals has dropped sharply. Hundreds of animals have become **extinct**. That means that there are no more of that kind of animal. For example, the dodo was a large, flightless bird that is now extinct. Many other animals are **endangered species**. This means there are very few left. Bald eagles, whooping cranes, the California condor, and blue whale are all endangered species. These are just a few of the many animals that are in danger of becoming extinct.

Fishing, hunting, and trapping can all endanger animal species. Another problem is the clearing away of plant life, such as forests. This destroys the homes of animals. And without the means for getting food, many animals die.

The Earth's ecosystem is balanced. Each kind of plant and animal helps keep this balance. The more kinds of plants and animals, the healthier the ecosystem. So each time any kind of plant or animal dies off, our ecosystem becomes a little less balanced.

On the Cutting Edge

In California, biologists are trying to help the small population of condors. The number of condors is so low that scientists have been capturing them to protect them. At the San Diego Zoo, biologists are trying to mate male and female condors. A few baby chicks have been safely hatched. The biologists hope to return the condors to the wild in greater numbers. They hope to save them from extinction.

A condor and a baby condor chick

Sources of Energy

Almost 75 percent of the energy people use comes from fossil fuels. These fuels are mainly used in transportation and in heating buildings. But fossil fuels are non-renewable resources. At some point in the future, we will run out of coal, oil, and natural gas. For that reason, and because of pollution from burning fossil fuels, we must develop other energy sources.

Nuclear fission creates energy by splitting atoms apart. This produces a great deal of heat. The heat is used to drive machinery that makes electricity. However, there are many problems with this kind of energy. It is very costly, for one thing. Nuclear fission also produces very dangerous wastes. Scientists have not yet found a safe method of getting rid of these wastes.

Nuclear fusion is another kind of nuclear energy. It involves *joining* atoms rather than splitting them. Many scientists have high hopes for this source of energy in the future. They believe it may be much safer than nuclear fission. However, scientists have not yet found a way to control the energy created by nuclear fusion.

There is a lot of energy in moving water. Dams are built to store the energy in rivers. Some scientists are working on using the energy in waves and the tides. Windmills are used to capture the energy in wind. The dams and windmills convert the captured energy into electricity.

Volcanoes and hot springs prove that there is great heat under the crust of the Earth. In some places, this heat has been trapped and used for energy.

The sun is a limitless, clean resource. Energy from the sun can be collected by panels placed on the roof of a building. The heated panels warm water in pipes

The demand for energy is very great and growing all the time. What effect do you think this will have on the Earth's environment?

behind the panels. This hot water is piped throughout the building to provide heat. This kind of energy is called *solar energy*. It is still rather costly. And solar panels take up a great deal of space. But many believe solar power will be an important source of energy in the future.

A modern windmill

On the Cutting Edge

Earth is one big ecosystem. One country's air pollution becomes the world's air pollution. The same is true for water and other resources.

Many of the world's leaders are realizing that to solve environmental problems on Earth, all countries must work together. In June 1992, an Earth Summit meeting was held in Rio de Janeiro, Brazil. Leaders from countries around the world talked about how they can work together to solve environmental problems.

Some say the meeting was a good beginning. The fact that countries are starting to talk about the environment is a step in the right direction.

Chapter Review

Chapter Summary

- Natural resources are all the things on Earth that people need to live. Minerals, water, air, soil, forests, wildlife, and energy are all natural resources. Conservation is the wise use and protection of these resources.

- Water is a non-renewable resource: there is a limited amount on Earth. People use great amounts of water every day. These uses often lead to water pollution. Factory wastes, farm fertilizers, and human sewage are some of the biggest water pollutants.

- Air is also a non-renewable resource. Factories and cars are the biggest air polluters. Some air pollutants are solid particles. Others are poisonous gases, such as sulfur. Acid rain is a result of sulfur in the air.

- Topsoil is bits of rock and the remains of plants and animals mixed together. All plants grow in topsoil. Erosion is the wearing away of topsoil by wind and rain. This can be controlled by planting ground covers, rotating crops, and planting windbreaks.

- As the human population grows, many kinds of animals and plants have become extinct. This has been caused by fishing, hunting, trapping, and the clearing away of plant life, such as forests. As more organisms become extinct, the balance of Earth's ecosystem becomes more endangered.

- About 75 percent of our energy comes from fossil fuels. Nuclear fission, dams, windmills, heat under the Earth's crust, and the sun are other sources of energy.

Chapter Quiz

Write the answers to the following questions on a separate sheet of paper.

1. Name six natural resources.
2. What are three ways that water gets polluted?
3. What is one way you could help cut back on air pollution?
4. What causes the erosion of topsoil?
5. What is one thing a farmer can do to control erosion?
6. Why might cutting down lots of forest land lead to the extinction of some animals?
7. What source of energy is most used today? Why might this be a problem in the future?

Renewable and Non-renewable Resources

Make a chart like the one below on a separate sheet of paper. Fill in the chart using the following resources.

| sunshine | soil | trees | minerals |
| air | water | fish | fossil fuels |

Renewable Resources	Non-renewable Resources

Mad Scientist Challenge: Recycling

Cans, bottles, plastic, and paper can all be recycled. Using these materials over and over again saves resources.

Find out if there is a recycling program in your area. On a separate sheet of paper, write a short report on how the program works. Answer the following questions:

Who collects cans, bottles, and paper in your area?

Where do they store what they collect?

How do they recycle these items for future use?

Chapter 25

Evolution: Changes in Life Over Time

The fierce tyrannosaurus rex died out about 65 million years ago. Why aren't there still dinosaurs alive today?

Chapter Learning Objectives

- Explain the theory of evolution.
- Describe the process of natural selection.
- Identify fossil evidence for evolution.

Words to Know

evolution   the gradual change in a species over time

fossils   the remains of organisms that lived long ago

natural selection   the way that those organisms best suited to their environment survive and pass their helpful traits along to offspring

paleontology   the scientific study of fossils

species   any group of organisms that can reproduce together

Not too long ago, scientists found the remains of a huge animal deep in a glacier. Its body had been preserved by the ice. It looked much like a hairy elephant. The animal, extinct for thousands of years, was a woolly mammoth.

What happened to the woolly mammoths? Are today's elephants their distant cousins? Why do some kinds of plants and animals become extinct? How do new ones come into being? In this chapter you will learn how living things change over time.

What Is Evolution?

Most plant and animal species change over time. A **species** is a group of organisms that can reproduce together. This slow, gradual change is called **evolution**. In the case of evolution, "slow" usually means thousands to millions of years.

You have read about the first specks of life on Earth. Scientists believe they appeared in the oceans about 3 billion years ago. All the organisms that have lived on the Earth since then evolved from those first creatures. The process of evolution goes on and on.

During the last few million years, hundreds of species have become extinct. And hundreds of others have developed. How do we know all of this? Is there any evidence to support the theory of evolution?

Fossil Evidence for Evolution

Fossils give much of the evidence for evolution. A **fossil** is any remaining part of a plant or animal that lived long ago.

Most living things never become fossils. Their bodies decay quickly after they die. To become a fossil, an organism must be preserved. There are several ways this can happen.

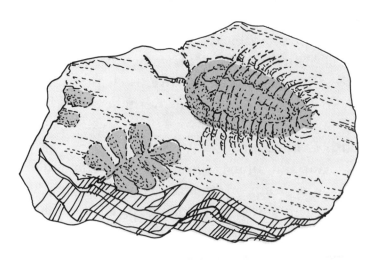

Fossils

The woolly mammoth, found frozen in the ice of Siberia, is one example of a fossil. The ice preserved parts of the body. Even some flesh and hair remained on the woolly mammoth!

Insects have been preserved in tree sap which hardened around the insect. Scientists can study these insects.

The teeth and bones of animals are mostly made of minerals. These do not decay as easily as cell tissue. Scientists have found bone fossils as old as 100,000,000 years.

Many fossils form on the bottom of lakes, seas, and swamps. Organisms die and sink to the bottom. They become buried in mud and sand. After thousands of years, the lakes, seas, and swamps dry up. The mud and sand harden into rock. The outlines of the organisms are left in the rock. Scientists study these shapes and imprints. The scientific study of fossils is called **paleontology**.

Scientists use fossils as clues to trace the course of life on Earth.

What Scientists Can Learn from Fossils

The Earth is made up of layers and layers of rock. You can see this at the Grand Canyon. There, a river has cut a deep gash through the layers of rock. You can see the different colors of rock in stripes along the canyon walls. The bottom layers are the oldest. The upper layers are the youngest.

Scientists learn how organisms change through time by studying fossils from different layers of rock. They discovered that the first living organisms on Earth were very simple. These simple organisms seemed to have gradually changed or evolved. They became more complex. That is, they developed more body parts and systems. Scientists can see how organisms from millions of years ago have evolved into the organisms of today.

Man is the most complex animal. So modern man was among the last animals to evolve.

For example, horses today appear to have evolved from an animal about the size of a fox. The horse slowly got longer legs. The original horse had four toes. The modern horse has one toe, or hoof. The hoof carries the greater weight of the modern horse better. This helps the modern horse to run faster.

Scientists have also learned that the Earth has undergone great changes in climate. Fossils of palm trees and other tropical plants have been found in Greenland in the far north!

Evolution of the horse

People in Biology: Charles Darwin

Scientists know that organisms change over time. But why do they change? A man named Charles Darwin has given an answer to this question.

Charles Darwin

In 1831, at the age of 22, Charles Darwin took a job on a ship called the HMS *Beagle*. He was the ship's scientist. For five years he studied the plants and animals he found as they sailed around the world. Darwin collected samples and took many notes. When he got home, he spent many more years trying to make sense of what he'd observed.

Darwin saw that different species of plants and animals were related. He knew that new species were appearing. And he knew that other species were becoming extinct. But he wanted to discover how that took place. In 1859, he published his findings. His book was called *On the Origin of Species by Means of Natural Selection.*

Another biologist named Alfred Wallace came up with the same ideas as Darwin, at the same time. In fact, the two men wrote letters back and forth about these ideas. This often happens in science. All ideas arise from other ideas. Darwin and Wallace both studied the work of many other biologists. Evolution is actually a very complex theory that continues to change and expand in our time. Biologists continue to study the ideas of Darwin and Wallace.

Biology Practice

Write the answers to the following questions on a separate sheet of paper.

1. What is the meaning of the word "evolution"?
2. What kinds of fossils have been found in Greenland?
3. About how long did it take Darwin to come up with his theory of evolution?

Jean Baptiste de Lamarck

People in Biology: Jean Baptiste de Lamarck

In 1809, before Darwin, a Frenchman named Jean Baptiste de Lamarck came up with a theory of evolution. He believed that traits evolved by use and disuse. He gave the example of giraffes. Lamarck said that giraffes used to have short necks. But they stretched their necks to reach leaves. As they stretched, their necks became longer. Then the giraffes passed this longer neck trait on to their offspring. Over time, the necks of giraffes became longer and longer. Lamarck argued that animals acquired traits to survive. He thought that these acquired traits became part of the genetic code.

However, in 1870, August Weissmann, a German biologist, proved Lamarck wrong. Weissmann cut short the tails of some mice. He let the mice reproduce. Then he cut short the offspring's tails. He continued this for more and more offspring. Not one mouse was born with a short tail. Acquired traits did not become part of the genetic code.

The Main Points of Darwin's Theory

Darwin's theory of evolution has six main points:

1. *Most organisms give birth to more offspring than can survive.* Trees give off thousands of seeds. Only a very few of these will grow into trees. Fish also lay thousands of eggs. Only a few will grow into adult fish. If all the offspring of every organism lived, there would be no room on Earth. There certainly would not be enough food.

2. *Living things must struggle to exist.* There is not enough space or food on Earth for every organism born to live. Living things are always in a struggle to get what they need. Most do not survive long enough to have their own offspring. Only those who can get the necessities of life will survive. Only those who survive to have offspring will pass on their genetic code.

3. *The individuals in a species are somewhat different from one another.* Some animals get more useful genes than others. Some cats are faster runners than other cats. The color of some mice helps them blend into their environment more easily than the color of other mice. These differences among individuals in a species are very important to Darwin's theory of evolution.

4. *Organisms with traits best suited to the environment have a better chance of survival.* A fast cat will do better running from dogs than a slow cat. Mice that blend in with their environment are less likely to be seen by hawks—or other things that eat them. A strong wolf will get more food than a weak one.

5. *Those organisms best suited to their environment will pass their traits along to offspring.* Cats with traits for running slowly will not live long. Many may not live

If organisms don't adapt to the changes in the environment, they will perish. Think about the dinosaurs. What happened to them?

long enough to reproduce. On the other hand, fast-running cats will live longer. They will reproduce. The fast-running traits will be passed along to offspring. The same is true for the mice. White mice do not blend into a field well. Hawks will see them and eat them. They will not get much of a chance to reproduce. Brown mice, on the other hand, are harder to see. More of them will get a chance to reproduce. The "brown" trait will be passed along. The "white" trait may die out. The demands of nature select fast cats and brown mice over slow cats and white mice. That is why Darwin's theory is called **natural selection**.

6. *New species will develop.* The traits that help a species survive are called *favorable traits.* These are the traits that get passed along to offspring. Organisms with *unfavorable traits* often do not live to reproduce. Very slowly, over many, many years, a species can become completely different. This happens because favorable traits are passed along and unfavorable ones are dropped. Darwin explained that whole new species could evolve in this way.

How Traits Change Over Time

Darwin explained a lot about evolution. His theory of natural selection is widely accepted today. However, he did not explain *how* traits change over time. He knew that Lamarck's ideas about giraffe's necks were not correct. He knew that changes in traits were passed along. They were not gotten through using or not using a body part. But how were the traits passed along? The answer lies in the genetic code.

Remember that traits are passed along by genes. A *mutation* is a change in the gene that causes a new trait or characteristic. Mutations are passed along to offspring. Most mutations are harmful. They do not help the organism survive.

Once in a while, though, a mutation is helpful to an organism. Suppose a short-necked giraffe received a gene for a longer neck. It would be able to reach more leaves. The giraffe would pass this trait along to its offspring. The long-necked giraffes would have an advantage over the short-necked giraffes. In the struggle to get enough food, the long-necked giraffes would do better.

Mutations are simply accidents of nature. The ideas of genetics give more evidence for Darwin's theory of evolution.

Amazing Biology

Farmers use pesticides to kill insects that eat farm crops. But a few insects are immune to the pesticide. The surviving insects have offspring that are immune to pesticide. Now, entire populations of insects are immune to pesticides. Farmers must find new ways to stop them from destroying the crops.

Chapter Review

Chapter Summary

- Plants and animals have slowly changed over millions of years. Some species have died out. Other new ones have appeared. This slow, gradual change in the organisms living on Earth is called evolution.

- Several different kinds of fossils give evidence for evolution. Organisms have been fossilized in ice, tree sap, and stone. Teeth and bones of animals from long ago have been found.

- Scientists are able to date these fossils. They believe that all present organisms have evolved from past organisms.

- Organisms have gotten much more complex over time. Scientists have also discovered that the climate of Earth has changed a great deal.

- Charles Darwin came up with a theory that explains how evolution happens. 1) Most organisms give birth to more offspring than can survive. 2) Living things must struggle to exist. 3) The individuals in a species are somewhat different from one another. 4) Organisms with traits best suited to the environment have a better chance at survival. 5) Those organisms best suited to their environment will pass their traits along to offspring. 6) New species will develop.

- The genetic code explains how traits may change within a species. A mutation may occur in the genetic code. Usually a mutation is harmful to an organism. Once in a while the mutation is a helpful trait. The helpful trait is passed along to offspring. It lets the organism adapt better to its environment. The organism survives to pass the mutation on to its offspring.

Chapter Quiz

Write the answers to the following questions on a separate sheet of paper.

1. What is a species?
2. Describe two kinds of fossils that provide evidence for evolution.
3. What can biologists learn from the different layers of rock in the Earth?
4. Why do scientists think that the Earth has undergone great changes in climate?
5. What is Darwin's theory of evolution called?
6. Give two examples of organisms that produce more offspring than can survive.
7. What field of biology explains how traits change within a species?
8. Why do organisms with seriously unfavorable traits often not reproduce?
9. Why does a fast-running cat have an advantage over a slow-running cat?
10. What human features make us well-suited to our environment?

Reporting on Biology: Dinosaur Fossils

On a separate sheet of paper, write a short report on dinosaur fossils. Explain how scientists know there were dinosaurs, and tell what remains of dinosaurs today. Use an encyclopedia or get help from a librarian to find information.

Mad Scientist Challenge: Favorable Traits

Compare yourself to other organisms living on Earth. What favorable traits do you have as a human being? What unfavorable traits do you have as a human being? If you could be any other organism on Earth, what would you be and why?

Unit 6 Review

Answer the following questions on a separate sheet of paper.

1. What is an energy cycle?

2. What do decomposers do?

3. What is a food web?

4. How do clouds form?

5. How does pollution create acid rain?

6. What happens when an animal hibernates?

7. Name two ways animals avoid danger.

8. What is the difference between renewable and non-renewable resources?

9. How does natural selection promote favorable traits in a species?

10. What causes traits to change in the genetic code?

Appendix

Glossary

Appendix A: Careers in Biology

Appendix B: Hiring Institutions

Appendix C: Metric Conversion Chart

Appendix D: The Five Kingdoms

Appendix E: The Animal Kingdom

Appendix F: The Four Food Groups

Appendix G: Calories in Foods

Appendix H: Important Vitamins

Appendix I: Minerals

Index

Glossary

abdomen the end part of an insect's body

adrenaline a hormone that gives the body extra energy in times of fright, anger, or excitement

algae (singular, alga) plant-like protists. Many *algae* are seaweeds.

amphibians cold-blooded vertebrates that live part of their lives in water and part on land

appendages parts that stick out from an organism, such as arms, legs, wings, claws, and feelers

arachnids arthropods with four pairs of legs, such as spiders and scorpions

area the number of square units that a surface covers

arteries blood vessels that carry blood away from the heart

arthropods animals with exoskeletons, segmented bodies, and jointed appendages, such as insects and arachnids

asexual reproduction the process of one cell splitting to form two daughter cells

atom the smallest particle of matter

atria the upper chambers of the heart

axons the fibers on neurons that carry messages away from the cell

bacteria (singular, bacterium) simple one-celled organisms that are visible only through a microscope

behavior the way an organism responds to the environment; all the actions of an organism

biological clock a timing process in animals, perhaps controlled by hormones, that lets them know when to eat, sleep, mate, hibernate, and migrate

biology the study of living things

blade the broad flat part of a leaf

botany the study of plants

calorie the basic unit of food energy

capillaries tiny blood vessels through which nutrients, oxygen, and wastes are exchanged with body cells and air sacs in the lungs

cardiac muscle the muscle tissue that makes up the heart

cell membrane a thin protective covering around a cell

cells the tiny basic units of which all living things are made

cellulose a kind of carbohydrate that people cannot digest

cell wall a hard covering around plant cells

centimeter 1/100th of a meter

cerebellum the part of the brain that controls balance and the working together of the muscles

cerebrum the part of the brain that controls voluntary muscle movements, thinking, learning, memory, and the senses

characteristics the qualities of a living thing that make it unique

chlorophyll   a green substance within the chloroplasts in plant cells that traps sunlight

chloroplasts   the parts in a plant cell that store sunlight to make food

cholesterol   a waxy substance made by the body and also found in fatty foods

chromosomes   the parts of a cell that pass on the characteristics of living things to offspring

cilia   tiny hairs some protists use to move

classification   the system biologists use to group organisms by type

community   all the living things in one ecosystem

complex carbohydrates   foods such as whole grains, potatoes, and pasta that provide the body with slow-burning energy

condense   change from a gas into a liquid

conditioning   the way learned behavior is taught

conservation   the wise use and protection of natural resources

consumers   organisms that cannot make their own food and must eat other organisms

control   a known quantity by which to measure the subject of an experiment

coronary system   the part of the circulatory system that supplies oxygen to the heart

crustaceans   a group of arthropods, such as crabs and lobsters, that generally live in water

cytoplasm   a jellylike substance filling a cell

decay   to break down into smaller pieces

decomposers   organisms that eat dead organisms and wastes

dendrites   the fibers on neurons that carry messages into the cell

dermis   a thick layer of skin, under the epidermis, which contains nerves, hair roots, blood vessels, and sweat and oil glands

digestion   the process by which the body breaks food down into nutrients that can be absorbed by the cells

dinosaurs   a group of reptiles that died off millions of years ago

DNA   molecules in the nuclei of cells that make up chromosomes and serve as a "code" for an organism's traits

dominant traits   traits that are stronger in an organism's genetic code and more likely to appear in offspring

eardrum   the tightly stretched membrane inside the ear that is sensitive to sound

ecology   the study of how all living things relate to one another and their world

ecosystem   the series of relationships between a community of organisms and the environment

egg   the female sex cell

elements   the basic substances of which all matter is made

embryo   the developing young after it has attached itself to the uterus

endangered species   animals in danger of becoming extinct

energy   the ability to do work

environment   everything in the immediate world around you

enzyme   a substance that causes chemicals to change form in the body

epidermis   the outermost layer of skin

erosion   the wearing away of topsoil

esophagus   a tube behind the windpipe that carries food from the mouth to the stomach

evaporate   change from a liquid to a gas

evolution   the gradual change in a species over time

exoskeleton   a tough, stiff covering or shell around the body of an organism

experiment   a test to get information

extinct   no longer existing

fact   an idea that has been proven by experiments

fertilization   the joining of egg and sperm cells

fetus   the offspring after fertilization of the egg but before birth; the last part of the development of the embryo

fibrous roots   many small, thin roots

flagella   a long tail some one-celled organisms use to move

food chain   a grouping of organisms in which lower organisms are eaten by higher ones

food web   many food chains that cross over one another

fossils   the remains of organisms that lived long ago

frond   the leaf of a fern

fungi (singular, fungus)   organisms that have no chlorophyll, yet cannot move about like animals in search of food. Mushrooms, molds, and yeasts are *fungi*.

genes   the parts of the DNA molecule that control the development of specific traits

genetics   the study of how the characteristics of a living thing are passed along to its offspring

germination   the process by which an embryo develops and finally breaks out of the seed

gills   organs used by fish for getting oxygen from water

greenhouse effect   what happens when too much carbon-dioxide on Earth traps the sun's heat

habitat   the place where an organism lives

herbaceous stems   green, soft stems

heredity   the process by which traits are passed from parents to offspring

hibernation   a long rest during which an animal's heartbeat and breathing rate slow down. Many animals *hibernate* through the entire winter.

hormones   the chemical messengers in the body that are produced by certain glands

host   animal on or in which parasites live

humus the organic matter in soil

instinct behavior that is known from birth

invertebrates animals without backbones

involuntary muscle a muscle that moves automatically, without your thinking about it

iris the colored part of the eye surrounding the pupil

joints the places in the body where two or more bones are joined, usually in a way that allows them to move

kilometer 1000 meters

lens a curved glass used in microscopes

ligaments bands of tissue that hold bones together at the joints

loam soil that has a good mixture of sand, clay, and humus

magnify to make something appear larger

mammals highly developed, warm-blooded animals, covered with fur or hair, that are fed milk from their mothers

marrow the soft center of bones where red blood cells are made

measurement the size, quantity, or amount found by measuring

medulla the part of the brain that controls automatic body functions such as involuntary muscle movements

menopause the time in a woman's life when she stops menstruating

menstruation the monthly shedding of blood from a woman's uterus

meter the standard unit of length in the metric system, equal to 39.4 inches, or slightly more than 3-1/4 feet

metric units the standard units of measurement in the metric system, based on the number ten and multiples of ten

microbiology the study of living things too small to see with the naked eye

microscope a device for viewing objects that are too small to be seen with the naked eye

microscopic too small to be seen with the naked eye

migration the way in which some animals travel long distances from season to season for feeding, nesting, and warmth

millimeter 1/1000th of a meter

minerals non-living substances found in small amounts in certain foods

mitochondria structures in a cell that convert food into energy

mitosis the process of cell reproduction

molecule two or more atoms joined together

mollusks animals with soft bodies that are not divided into segments, such as snails, oysters, and clams. Most *mollusks* have hard shells.

monera (singular, moneran) tiny organisms that have some nucleic materials, but no true nuclei, in their cells, such as bacteria

mutation a change in the genetic code, causing an abnormality in the organism

mutualism a symbiotic relationship in which both partners are helped

natural resources the things on Earth that people need to live

natural selection the way that those organisms best suited to their environment survive and pass their helpful traits along to offspring

nectar a sweet liquid in flowers that attracts insects

neurons nerve cells throughout the body that carry signals to and from the brain

niche the job function of an organism within an ecosystem

nitrates a form of nitrogen that can be used by cells for making proteins

nitrogen-fixing changing nitrogen gas into a usable form for life

non-renewable resources resources that are in limited supply

nonvascular plants plants that do not have structures for transporting water

nucleus (plural, nuclei) the part of a cell that controls all the other parts

nutrients the substances in foods that organisms need for energy

offspring the young of a living thing

organ a group of tissues working together, such as a heart or kidney

organism any living thing

ovaries the female organs that make egg cells and hormones

oviducts the tubes through which egg cells travel to the uterus

ovulation the monthly release of an egg cell from an ovary

paleontology the scientific study of fossils

parasites organisms that live on or inside other organisms

penis the male organ that delivers sperm to the female

petals the parts of a flower that are often brightly colored

petiole a thin rib that connects the leaf to the plant

pheromones the chemical signals some animals use to affect or attract other animals of the same species

phloem a special tissue in roots and stems that carries food down the plant

photosynthesis the process by which plant cells make food from sunlight, water, and carbon dioxide

pistil the female part of a flower

placenta the structure through which food, oxygen, and wastes pass between the mother and the embryo

plant embryo the early, undeveloped state of a new plant

plant ovary the flower part, at the bottom of the pistil, where egg cells are formed

plasma the liquid part of blood

platelets solids in blood plasma that help to make blood clot

pollen in some plants, yellow grains that hold sperm

pollination the process by which pollen reaches the pistil in a flower

pollution any foreign substance harmful to the ecosystem

population   the group of one kind of organism living in an ecosystem

primates   a group of mammals that includes apes, gorillas, and humans

producers   organisms that make food by using energy from the sun

proteins   nutrients in foods that build body tissues

protists   tiny one-celled organisms that are neither plants nor animals but that often have characteristics of both

protozoans   animal-like protists

pseudopods   a kind of arm amebas use to move

pupil   the black circle in the center of the eye

receptor cells   body cells that receive outside information

recessive traits   traits that are weaker in an organism's genetic code and less likely to appear in offspring

recycle   to use again

reflex   an automatic and involuntary response to an outside stimulus

renewable resources   resources that can be resupplied

reproduction   the way organisms make more of their own kind

reservoirs   lakes that people build to save water

respiration   the process by which cells get energy from food and oxygen

respond   to act according to conditions in the environment

retina   the light-sensitive layer of receptor cells at the back of the eyeball

root hairs   tiny hair-like structures on roots that absorb water into the plant

saliva   a liquid in the mouth that aids digestion

semen   the mixture of fluids in which sperm leaves the body

semi-permeable   having tiny pores so that certain molecules can pass through

sepals   the green leaf-like parts of a flower that support the petals

sexual reproduction   the joining of two sex cells, a sperm and an egg, to produce offspring

skeleton   a group of bones that work together to support an organism's body

soil   the top layer of the Earth's surface, made up of rocks, minerals, water, air, and decayed plant and animal matter

species   any group of organisms that can reproduce together

specimen   something that is looked at under a microscope

sperm   a male sex cell

spinal cord   a rope of neurons that connects the brain and the nervous system

spores   reproductive cells of organisms such as ferns, fungi, and algae

stamens   the male parts of a flower

stomata (singular, stoma)   tiny pores on leaves that allow gases in and out of the leaves

synapses   the spaces between neurons

system a group of organs working together

taproot one thick root

taste buds receptor cells on the tongue that are sensitive to taste

tendons bands of tissue that attach muscles to bones

testes the male organs that produce sperm cells

theory an idea that has not been proven with experiments

thorax the middle part of an insect's body

tissue a group of cells that all do the same job

topsoil the upper layer of rich, dark soil in which plants grow

traits characteristics, which may be inherited, that identify organisms as individuals

unit a fixed amount or quantity that is used as a standard of measurement

universe everything that exists, including the Earth, sun, planets, stars, and outer space

urethra the tube through which urine (and in males, also sperm) leaves the body

uterus the female organ in which a fertilized egg develops into a baby

vacuoles openings in a cell that store food, water, or wastes

vagina the canal that leads to a woman's uterus

vascular plants plants that have structures for transporting water

veins blood vessels that carry blood toward the heart

ventricles the lower chambers of the heart

vertebrates animals with backbones

villi (singular, villus) tiny finger-shaped structures in the walls of the small intestine that absorb digested food into the blood

virus a microscopic "organism" that causes diseases and is missing some cell parts. *Viruses* can grow and reproduce only in certain living cells.

vitamins living substances found in certain foods that the body needs to function properly and to resist diseases

volume the amount of space an object occupies

voluntary muscle a muscle that moves when you decide to move it

wastes the leftover matter a cell or body does not need after it uses food for energy

woody stems hard brown stems, including tree trunks

xylem a special tissue in roots and stems that carries water up the plant

zoology the study of animals

zygote the cell that forms right after an egg cell has been fertilized

Appendix A

Careers in Biology

Anatomist
Animal ecologist
Biochemist
Biological photographer
Biomedical engineer
Biophysicist
Botanist
Dietician
Doctor
Editor
Environmental analyst
Environmental scientist
Food-and-drugs inspector
Forester
Geneticist
Hospital worker
Hygienist
Laboratory assistant
Marine biologist
Medical illustrator
Medical librarian
Microbiologist
Oceanographer
Optometrist
Pathologist
Physical therapist
Plant pathologist
Scientific artist
Soil scientist
Taxidermist
Teacher
Veterinarian
Writer
Zoologist

Appendix B

Hiring Institutions

Aquariums
Arboretums
Botanical gardens
Business corporations
Colleges and schools
Consulting firms
Cosmetic companies
Doctors' offices
Government agencies
    Agricultural Department
    Environmental Protection Agency
    Fish and Wildlife Service
    Health and Human Services Department
    National Institute of Health
    National Science Foundation
    Peace Corps
Hatcheries
Hospitals
Libraries and research foundations
Medical clinics and laboratories
Medical-supply companies
Museums
National and state parks
Nurseries
Publishers
Zoological parks

Appendix C

Metric Conversion Chart

Length
1 millimeter = .03937 inch
1 centimeter = .3937 inch
1 decimeter = 3.937 inches
1 meter = 39.37 inches = 3.281 feet = 1.0936 yards
1 kilometer = 1,093.6 yards = .6214 mile
1 inch = 2.54 centimeters
1 foot = 30.48 centimeters = .3048 meter
1 yard = 91.44 centimeters = .9144 meter
1 mile = 160,933 centimeters = 1,609.33 meters = 1.60933 kilometers

Area
1 square millimeter = .00155 square inch
1 square centimeter = .155 square inch
1 square decimeter = 15.5 square inches
1 square meter = 1,550 square inches = 10.764 square feet = 1.196 square yards
1 square inch = 6.4516 square centimeters
1 square foot = 929.03 square centimeters
1 square yard = .8361 square meters

Volume
1 cubic inch = 16.387 cubic centimeters
1 cubic foot = 28.317 cubic centimeters = .0283 cubic meter
1 cubic yard = 764,553 cubic centimeters = .7646 cubic meter
1 fluid ounce = 29.573 milliliters
1 quart = .9643 liter
1 gallon = 3.7853 liters
1 liter = 1.0567 quarts

Weight
1 gram = .035 ounce
1 kilogram = 2.2 pounds
1 metric ton = 2,200 pounds

Appendix D

The Five Kingdoms	Kingdom	Description	Examples
	Moneran	Single-celled Has no cell nuclei	Bacteria Blue-green algae
	Protist	Most are single-celled Has a nuclei	Protozoans Algae
	Fungus	Many-celled Cannot move Has no chlorophyll Has cell walls	Yeasts Molds Mushrooms Mildew
	Plant	Many specialized cells Uses chlorophyll and sunlight to make food Has cell walls	Seed plants Ferns Mosses
	Animal	Eats other organisms Has no chlorophyll Many specialized cells Cannot make its own food	Insects Mammals Birds Fish

Appendix E

The Animal Kingdom Main Groups Characteristics		
Sponges	Body has canals and pores Gets food and oxygen from water washing through it	
Jellyfish, corals, and sea anemones	Sack-like body Tentacles with stinging cells	

Flatworms
  (tapeworms)
  (planariums)
	Flat body
	Simple structure
	Many are parasites	

Roundworms
  (trichina)
	Smooth, round body with
	    tapered ends
	Simple digestive system	

Segmented worms (earthworms)	Segmented body Most complex of the worms	

Mollusks
  (oysters)
  (clams)
  (snails)
  (squid)
	Soft body
	Most have hard shells	

Spiny skinned
  (starfish)
  (sea urchins)
  (sand dollars)
	Tough spiny covering
	Many have rays or arms	

Arthropods
  (insects)
  (spiders)
  (crustaceans)
	Exoskeleton
	Segmented body
	Jointed appendages	

Chordates
  (all the
  vertebrates)
	Have backbone	

Appendix F

The Five Food Groups

Food Group	Sample Foods	Main Nutrient Contributions
Meat and meat substitutes	Beef, pork, lamb, fish, poultry, eggs, nuts, legumes	Protein, iron, riboflavin, niacin, thiamine
Dairy products	Milk, buttermilk, yogurt, cheese, cottage cheese, soy milk, ice cream	Calcium, protein, riboflavin, thiamine
Fruits	Apples, bananas, grapes, kiwis, melons, oranges, pears, pineapples	Vitamin A, Vitamin C, thiamine, iron, riboflavin
Vegetables	Broccoli, celery, carrots, cabbage, lettuce, peas, potatoes, radishes	Vitamin A, Vitamin C, thiamine, iron, riboflavin
Grains (bread and cereal products)	All whole-grain and enriched flours and products	Riboflavin, iron, thiamine, niacin

Appendix G

Calories in Foods

chocolate milk shake (8 ounces)	421
diet cola (6 ounces)	1
regular cola (6 ounces)	78
orange juice (8 ounces)	110
skim milk (8 ounces)	90
whole milk (8 ounces)	150
bran muffin	113
pizza with cheese (one piece)	185
spaghetti with tomato sauce and cheese (one cup)	260
ice cream (one big scoop)	150–250
egg (one, poached)	80
apple, fresh	70
banana, fresh	100
strawberries (one-half cup)	30
hot dog	170
carrots, fresh (one-half cup)	25
lettuce (five leaves)	25
potato (large, baked)	100
french fries (20)	300
hamburger patty (3 ounces)	225
fruit pie (one piece)	400
cheese, cheddar (one-inch cube)	70
chicken, fried (half breast)	155
chocolate bar (3 ounces)	450
split pea soup (one cup)	145
French salad dressing (1 tablespoon)	45
baked fish, sole (3-1/2 ounces)	200

Appendix H

Important Vitamins	Vitamin	Source	Body Function
	A	Leafy and yellow vegetables, egg yolk, milk, liver, butter, margarine	Good eyesight, healthy skin and hair, growth
	B_1	Whole grains, yeast, milk, green vegetables, egg yolk, liver, fish, soybeans, peas	Strong heart, nerves, and muscles; growth; respiration
	B_2	Lean meat, wheat germ, yeast, milk, cheese, eggs, liver, bread, leafy green vegetables	Healthy skin, growth, good eyesight, reproduction
	B_{12}	Liver, lean meat, milk, fresh fish, egg yolk, green vegetables, shellfish	Making blood, helping nervous system
	C	Oranges, grapefruit, lemons, limes, berries, vegetables, tomatoes	Healthy bones, strong blood vessels, preventing sickness, healing of wounds
	D	Egg yolk, milk, fresh fish	Strong teeth and bones, growth
	E	Leafy green vegetables, wheat germ, oils	Aids fertility
	K	Vegetables, soybeans	Helps blood clotting

Appendix I

Minerals	Mineral	Source	Body Function
	Calcium	Milk, vegetables, meats, dried fruits, whole-grain cereals	Healthy bones and teeth, blood clotting, prevention of muscle spasms
	Iodine	Saltwater fish, shellfish, iodized salt	Functioning of thyroid gland, regulation of use of energy in cells
	Iron	Liver, meats, eggs, nuts, dried fruits, leafy green vegetables	Formation of red blood cells
	Magnesium	Milk, meats, whole-grain cereals, peas, beans, nuts, vegetables	Normal muscle and nerve action, regulation of body temperature, building strong bones
	Phosphorus	Milk, meat, fish, poultry, nuts, vegetables, whole-grain cereals	Bone and teeth formation, nerve and muscle function, energy production
	Potassium and Sodium	Most foods, table salt (sodium)	Blood and cell functions, maintains balance of fluids in tissue

Index